SEMPER FI:

THE PSALMS OF ROBERT ALEXANDER

A Devotional Biography

Compiled by

ERIK PETTERSEN

This book, so lovingly put together by Robert's friend Erik, celebrates Robert's beautiful soul. Robert's courage, his profound faith, and unwavering love for his Creator are inspiring. May it be so for you and me...

Gerda

ISBN: 1-4033-4910-X (e-book)
ISBN 1-4033-4911-8 (Paperback)
ISBN: 1-4033-4912-6 (Dustjacket)

This book is printed on acid free paper.

1st Books - rev. 09/25/02

Acknowledgments

I am deeply indebted to a number of people for their assistance in compiling this book. Bonnie Haberman, Robert Alexander's younger sister, provided invaluable input about his early family and school life. Fred Hachmeister, one of his college roommates at Lafayette, shared remembrances about Robert's academic and journalistic achievements during his time there. Jim Williams and Scott Warrick, both fellow warriors with Robert in the battle against prostate cancer, graciously shared their personal remembrances and impressions. Mark Papera, who was one of Robert's most devoted prayer partners during his last two years, allowed me to read and use his correspondence. Jim Small, who became Robert's close friend and confidante – and whom Robert called his Jonathan – became my friend, too. He offered unique insights during two meetings at his cabinetmaking shop, allowed me to use some of the cards he had received from Robert and graciously fielded a number of my follow-up phone calls. His personal diary helped keep my chronology straight.

As a first-time author, I benefited greatly from my colleagues in the Annapolis Fellowship of Christian Writers, under the leadership of Jeri Sweany. Jeri in turn was kind enough to refer me to Homer Dowdy, an accomplished author and Annapolis neighbor. Homer graciously became a much needed mentor, offering guidance and wise counsel during the development of my manuscript.

Most of all, though, I owe my heartfelt thanks to Gerda Alexander, who not only acquiesced to my request to compile Robert's writings, but who has been a valued collaborator every step of the way.

Erik Pettersen
Annapolis, Maryland

Dedicated to the memory of Homer Dowdy and Midshipman 1st Class Ken Neptun, who, like Robert Alexander, finished well.

"Be thou faithful unto death, and I will give thee a crown of life." Revelation 2:10 (KJV)

Table of Contents

Foreword

Despite the fact that we share the same surname, I had never met this book's namesake – until I began reading *The Psalms of Robert Alexander*.

Despite the fact that I've been personally acquainted with the compiler of Alexander's *Psalms*, Erik Pettersen, since the very beginning of my tenure in the fall of 2001 as the senior chaplain at the United States Naval Academy, I knew nothing of Erik's writing ability or his labor of love for what has become his first book – until I began reading *Psalms*.

As is the case in the biblical book of Psalms, these *Psalms* are the lyrics of a relationship between a finite man and the infinite God. In response to the question, "How shall we sing the Lord's song in a strange land?" (Psalm 137:4, KJV) Robert Alexander and Erik Pettersen provide cues through Robert's writings as he endured the affliction of prostate cancer.

It is the privilege – and Divine expectation – of every true follower of Jesus to become broken bread and poured out wine. For those of us who struggle with this imperative, whether theoretically or practically, *Psalms* is gentle encouragement to faithfulness in all things, and in all circumstances.

Chaplain Luther C. Alexander, Jr., USN
Annapolis, Maryland

Introduction

In July of 1996, Robert Alexander – Marine Corps veteran, insurance executive, devoted husband, committed Christian – was told that he had inoperable prostate cancer and that he had fourteen months to live. By dint of his considerable intellect, gritty determination, unwavering support from his loving wife Gerda and a growing faith, he lived four and a half more years and launched a ministry that literally touched thousands of people.

Two years after his initial diagnosis, Robert underwent a profound spiritual experience while attending a Promise Keepers gathering at Veterans Stadium in Philadelphia. Over the next year, he authored the writings that were the inspiration for this book. I am merely the compiler. I felt that the beauty of my friend's "psalms" needed to be shared, and, in the spring of last year, I broached the idea with Gerda. She graciously agreed. I am deeply indebted to her for her unstinting assistance.

Chapter 1: "What an Opportunity to Witness!"

> *"I believe that every time a non-Christian gets cancer, a Christian gets cancer. I believe that every time a non-Christian loses his job, a Christian loses his job...so the world can see the difference."* Stephen Brown[1]

Some years ago, a friend invited me to a luncheon at the old Robert Treat hotel in Newark, New Jersey. The speaker was the famed opera singer, Jerome Hines. In discussing his life, Hines shared some of his early trials, including the fact that, at the age of thirty-four, he had been diagnosed with cancer. He related how, when he confided his diagnosis to a Christian friend, the friend's response was, "How wonderful!" Very much taken aback, Hines asked his friend, "What do you mean?" To which his friend replied, "What an opportunity to witness!"

That recollection is brought vividly to mind when I reflect on the remarkable final years of my dear friend, Robert Alexander.

My first encounter with Robert was, by all appearances, totally unremarkable. One fall Sunday morning in 1992, he introduced himself to me on a back stairway of our church, where he and his wife Gerda had just begun worshiping. Soft-spoken, short, a bit pudgy, and impeccably dressed in a dark suit, he easily fit the stereotype of the insurance executive that he was. His close-cropped white-gray hair was the only hint that he was a Marine Corps veteran.

Over the next few years, Robert and I saw more and more of each other. We both sang in the choir and enjoyed learning Scripture in the context of great music. With other choir members, I became almost equally fond of his wife Gerda's incomparable chocolate mousse at our annual Christmas parties! Robert expressed interest and became involved in two evangelical Christian men's ministries with me, the Christian Business Men's Committee (CBMC) and Campus Crusade's Executive Ministries. And I became aware of his exceptional administrative capabilities as we worked together on a search committee to screen candidates and recruit a new minister of music for our church.

One summer morning in 1996, during one of our weekly CBMC group meetings, Robert confided that he had just been diagnosed with inoperable prostate cancer. I was naturally quite alarmed, as I had already experienced the loss of several friends and colleagues to this dread disease. But, outwardly at least, Robert expressed neither anger nor fear. He actually tried to comfort me by making light of it and saying, "Erik, this is one of the few exclusively male clubs left in America!" And he went on to suggest that perhaps God was defining a new area of ministry for him.

It wasn't until some time later that I learned Robert's initial prognosis – he had been given just fourteen months to live.

Robert and Gerda had already made some sensible post-retirement plans. These included a move from their home in a New Jersey suburb of New York to a continuing care retirement community (CCRC) just west of Harrisburg, Pennsylvania. They had signed a pre-construction contract, but now Robert's health posed an obvious complication. With characteristic honesty, they shared Robert's diagnosis with the administrators of the CCRC, affording them the opportunity to abrogate their agreement. Instead – and to their credit – the administrators agreed to honor it.

The New Jersey home that the Alexanders were leaving was what Robert called "an English cottage" and was somewhat unique. It had just one bedroom, and, early on, Robert expressed some concern about its marketability. So he collaborated with our 17-year-old son Matthew in designing and producing a descriptive brochure. It wasn't long before two prospective buyers emerged. They began a bidding war, with one offering more than the Alexanders' asking price. True to form, Gerda and Robert refused to accept more than they had asked for.

After the Alexanders moved to Newville, Pennsylvania in the fall of 1996, our contact was, for the most part, limited to e-mail messages and phone calls. But I became aware that Robert and Gerda had indeed identified a fertile new area of ministry – reaching out to men and families afflicted by prostate cancer. And this was not a half-hearted effort!

At Christmas time in 1998, Robert sent me an incredibly inspiring card that he had made. Its text gave clear evidence of profound spiritual growth, as well as of extraordinary inner strength. And it was beautifully expressed:

Glorious God, my Creator and Lord,
This day is all praise and thanks
For all my days.
I breathe and it is Your breath that fills me.
I look and it is Your light by which I see.
I move and it is Your energy moving in me.
I listen and even the stones speak of You.

I touch and You are between finger and skin.
I think and the thoughts are but sparks
from the fire of Your truth.
I love and the throb is Your presence.
I laugh and it is the rustle of Your passing.
I weep and Your Spirit broods over me.

I long and it is the tug of your kingdom.
I praise You,
Glorious Heavenly Father,
For this curious day,
For the impulses that have made it unique
To Gerda and to me,
For the gifts that grace it,
For the gladness that accompanies it.

I thank You for all the undeserved blessings
You have given us:
Each special person you have placed
Here in front of us this day, that we might
nurture and love them in Christ's name,
For the affliction you have given me and the
Comfort wherewith I may comfort those who
Also are afflicted.

I pause to praise and thank You
With this one more trip of words

Which leaves too much uncarried,
But not unfelt,
Unlived,
Unloved.
Thank you, my dearest Jesus,
My Lord, My God, My All in All!

Your Robert
December 31, 1998

My first reaction was that my friend had just written the 151st Psalm! But I soon learned that, since attending a Promise Keepers gathering in Philadelphia during the preceding summer, Robert had written a number of "psalms." He wrote them at his high points and at his low points. He incorporated many of them – particularly psalms of encouragement – into countless cards that he sent to the men and families to whom he was ministering.

For the next two years, whenever I encountered people who were affected by prostate cancer, I immediately referred them to Robert. He responded graciously to each one. A new friend I met through Robert's ministry was an Annapolis neighbor, Ray Goff. Like Robert, Ray was – and still is! – both a prostate cancer survivor and a Marine Corps veteran. He and Robert became fast and close e-mail friends and often copied me on their messages to one another, always closing with the Marines' time honored salutation, "Semper Fi."

Semper Fideles – always faithful – is a most fitting descriptor of my friend Robert Alexander, whose faithfulness to his beloved Corps was surpassed by his faithfulness to his Lord and Savior, Jesus Christ.

Chapter 2: "It's Robert!"

> *"Train up a child in the way he should go; and when he is old, he will not depart from it."* Proverbs 22:6 (KJV)

Robert Harold Alexander was born in Philadelphia on August 13, 1927, the first son from the marriage of John Alexander and Helen Thompson. John was a graduate of Temple University and a highly successful physical education teacher. He coached a number of championship teams and ultimately became Supervisor of Physical and Health Education for the entire Philadelphia school district. Helen was a graduate of The Philadelphia Museum College of Art and worked as an art teacher in the public school system.

The Alexanders took their parenting roles seriously. As professional educators, they placed a strong emphasis on their children's reading and other academic endeavors. They insisted on proper speech and good manners and encouraged their children to learn to play a musical instrument. When necessary, they made budgetary sacrifices to pay for lessons. The family attended church regularly, said grace before every meal and offered prayers at bedtime each night. On Sunday afternoons, after worship and a filling mid-day meal, they often drove through the rolling hills of the surrounding countryside, visiting friends and members of their extended family. When the school year ended, John and Helen ran a summer camp in nearby Downington. The children participated, too, beginning as campers and eventually progressing to become counselors.

This wholesome family life gave Robert a strong foundation. He particularly enjoyed reading, perhaps even more so than his siblings, and this interest extended to his study of the Bible. He was extremely observant, had an eye for detail and shared his mother's love for artistic beauty. These traits found expression in very creative and complex stories and letters, which he wrote even as a little child. At the same time, he sought to achieve his father's approval through more physical "manly" pursuits. Though not a natural athlete, Robert exhibited a tenacity that inspired his sister Bonnie. She recalls that he thrived on overcoming challenges and that for many years a motivating quotation hung in a frame on the wall of his room:

> "Nothing in the world can take the place of Persistence.
> Talent will not; nothing is more common than unsuccessful men with talent.
> Genius will not; unrewarded genius is almost a proverb.
> Education will not; the world is full of educated derelicts.
> Persistence and determination alone are omnipotent."

Her research attributed the quote to Calvin Coolidge, who, in 1932, distributed it as a broadside to agents of the New York Life Insurance Company.

Like most older brothers, Robert could also be imaginatively mischievous. On more then one occasion, he was known to send witches' voices through an air vent in his younger sister's room to have her do his bidding.

In 1939, with their family having grown to include two sons and three daughters, the Alexanders moved to the Philadelphia suburb of Ridley Park. They enrolled their children in the town's public schools, and Robert initially encountered difficulty in adapting to his new surroundings. The situation was exacerbated by some of the faculty. His math teacher told him that he would "never get it." But as he recalled this in later life, Robert chuckled with satisfaction that he had gone on to work with statistics. The school coach openly expressed his disappointment that the son of Jack Alexander, a coach of championship teams, wasn't particularly strong or athletically inclined. Yet, with characteristic persistence, Robert was to prove himself through rigorous physical training and service in the Marine Corps.

Robert found a kindred spirit, though, in his English teacher, Miss Hipps. She helped her new pupil continue to develop his love for words and expressive ways to convey ideas. But her most important contributions may have been in recognizing how special her new student was and in providing an inspirational environment in which he could grow.

Upon his graduation from Ridley Park High School in 1945, Robert enrolled at nearby West Chester State Teachers College, majoring in secondary education. He defrayed the cost by working for a florist and delivering flowers by bicycle. But he appeared to lack direction and left West Chester in 1947. He then obtained employment at a succession of local companies, including a cable manufacturing firm and a shipping company. On April 1, 1948, while working for the General Coal Company in Philadelphia, he enlisted in the Marine Corps Reserve. He was called up to active duty on August 30, 1950, shortly after the outbreak of hostilities in Korea and his twenty-third birthday. He reported to Parris Island, South Carolina for boot camp. On July 23, 1951, he was assigned to the Marine detachment aboard the aircraft carrier *USS Midway* (CVB-41), which made a deployment to the Mediterranean the following January. Shortly after leaving Norfolk, the ship encountered a major storm. On January 25, after their safe arrival off of Gibraltar, Robert recounted some of the excitement in a letter to his parents:

> "....We didn't have any foul weather until our second or third day out. Then it began! During the next four days we really had rough going. No one was allowed on the weather decks because of the high seas, and flight operations were cancelled as well as gunnery exercises. During the fifth evening a shock wave ripped the shields off #11 and #13 three-inch gun mounts, completely exposing them to the seas. Mounts #9 and #7 (mine) weren't touched by the storm..."

The Med deployment lasted into the summer, and Robert advanced rapidly. By March 1, 1952, he had been promoted to the rank of Staff Sergeant (E-6). In August he was selected to attend the Officer Candidate School (OCS) Screening Course in Quantico, Virginia. But he was beginning to sense a different calling. Nearly fifty years later, he was to recall a significant spiritual experience while attached to the *Midway*:

> "I remember well an earlier turning point in my life as a young Marine, traveling back to my ship at the Norfolk naval base from weekend liberty. I was sitting in the back seat of a busload of snoring sailors, thumbing through my new copy of the Amplified New Testament with the aid of a flashlight. There that verse was, waiting to be discovered....to be believed....to be put into action. Philippians 3:10 said all I needed to hear:
>
> *'[For my determined purpose is] that I may know Him – that I may progressively become more deeply and intimately acquainted with Him, perceiving and recognizing and understanding [the wonders of His Person] more strongly and more clearly. And that I may in that same way come to know the power outflowing from His resurrection [which it exerts over believers]; and that I may so share in His sufferings as to be continually transformed [in spirit unto His likeness even] to His death.'*
>
> "I heard it then and it changed me, my service career, and my choice in education..."

Robert was anxious to make up for lost time and resume his education. He applied to, and was accepted by, Lafayette College in Easton, Pennsylvania, which he was to attend on the GI Bill. Upon separation from active duty on October 10, 1952, he proceeded directly to Lafayette, arriving a few weeks after the start of the fall semester. With his intellect and motivation, it didn't take him long to catch up.

Robert majored in history and excelled in his academic work. He was also very active in extracurricular activities: he joined the Phi Gamma Delta fraternity; participated in Alpha Phi Omega, the national service fraternity; served as manager of the Lafayette track team; and was awarded a Medal of Merit from Pi Delta Epsilon, the honorary collegiate journalism fraternity, after serving as Editor of the college yearbook. He was selected for inclusion in *Who's Who Among Students in American Colleges and Universities* and chosen as his class' lifetime president. Fred Hachmeister, one of Robert's Lafayette roommates, remembers him as being "studious, articulate and precise," characteristics that he retained throughout his life. Robert enhanced these impressions by smoking a pipe. Fred recalls that he also had a "bulldog grip" and that he could never seem to throw anything out.

Convicted by the message of Philippians 3:10, Robert became heavily involved with the church on campus. This was confirmed by a document Gerda found, stating that he had been elected a ruling elder of the Lafayette College Presbyterian Church on May 10, 1953, at the tender age of twenty-five!

By applying the credits he had already earned at West Chester, Robert was able to complete his degree requirements by the spring of 1955. In fact, he was graduated with distinction and earned a one-year Rockefeller Fellowship to Yale's Berkeley Divinity school. During the intervening summer, he worked in Lafayette's Admissions Office. At Yale he continued to excel academically, earning four A's and one B. Upon leaving Yale in 1956, he was recruited by his national fraternity, Phi Gamma Delta, to be their field secretary in Washington, DC. After serving in this capacity for several years, Robert accepted a teaching position at the Friends Central School in Philadelphia. But he still appeared uncertain about the direction for his life.

In 1960, while teaching at Friends, Robert completed a psychological profile called the Szondi Test and submitted it to Pennsylvania Hospital for evaluation. Although he appears to have given the evaluators the firm impression that he was submitting it on behalf of someone else, the hospital's report leaves no doubt in Gerda's mind – nor in mine – that Robert had completed the test for himself! Gerda is struck by the remarkably accurate insights into the man she was to marry[2]:

> "Dear Mr. Alexander:
>
> "Herewith our analysis of the Szondi Test material which you forwarded us recently. We understand that the test patterns are those of a male individual between 25 and 30 years of age....
>
> "The material indicates that from the standpoint of basic emotional drives, there is very definite maturity, and a capacity to sublimate crude affective energies towards cultural and intellectual action. There is a residual indecision, however, with respect to the individual's receptive needs for approval, acceptance and affection. Because of this

residual fluctuation, there is a tendency in this individual towards sensitivity and occasionally work inefficiency, particularly in areas calling for persistent precision.

"The projection material presents an ego organization which is seen only in individuals of superior intelligence. It is one in which the individual is very sensitive to external challenges or threats to the maintenance of a rather strong narcissistic egocenticity. It is a pattern implying the individual to focus on intellectual levels. He is a rationalizer, an intellectualizer, and he would tend to utilize these capacities to fulfill his needs for recognition, importance, and his drive toward assuming a pedestal in life. This is also a picture in which the individual could be a bit contentious in a 'doubting Thomas' fashion. There would be times when he would be a bit insensitive to the feelings of others in the pursuit of his fulfillment.

"Motivational patterns are those of the idealist. The implication here is that he would have some difficulties in achieving concrete, or materialistic success. He is positively motivated with respect to social relationships, even though his ego organization would tend to foster a bit of coolness in such relationships. The implication is that he would be successful from the standpoint of general social relationships.

> "The overall patterns are those of an individual who would be moved towards a humanitarian vocation on an intellectual plane. He would be interested in improving his fellow man. Despite the egocentricity seen here, there is much capacity for empathy, for understanding, and for self sacrificing hard work.
>
> "I hope the above interpretations will be of interest to you. Needless to say, we would be interested in learning whether or not the patterns seen here concur with your knowledge of the individual who undertook the test."

The letter was signed by the hospital's Supervisor of Reeducation. It is impossible to know what impact this report had on him, but some time after this, Robert embarked on a career in the insurance industry. Perhaps he recognized personal traits in himself that President Coolidge had found lacking in those industry executives back in 1932!

Now well into his thirties, Robert was still single. The possibility and timing of matrimonial union had become a source of constant speculation by his family. Although he dated a number of women, he seemed to find more in common with their mothers, who were no doubt impressed by his maturity and manners. It might be surmised that, for his part, Robert connected with them on an intellectual plane that overshadowed their daughters.

Then, in 1967, while working for the A.M. Best Company in Morristown, New Jersey, Robert took special notice of a young German colleague named Gerda Herden, who worked on the other side of the floor. Gerda recalls their first date following a company Christmas party in 1968. After the party, Robert offered to take her to dinner, and Gerda accepted. When they returned to the hotel, they talked for another two hours. Gerda found herself attracted to this man with the quiet yet determined demeanor. She vividly remembers Robert saying, "We both know it. We belong together!" And he was right!

Robert and Gerda were engaged in July 1969 and married three months later, on October 11. On their honeymoon, they went to the five-star Hershey Hotel, in Robert's beloved Pennsylvania countryside. They returned to New Jersey and began their life together in an apartment in Morristown. John and Helen Alexander were smitten with their new daughter-in-law, too, and there were many reciprocal visits. Gerda had made their son's life complete, and they admired her fierce loyalty and devotion to him.

In 1972, Robert and Gerda purchased their first house, in Clinton, New Jersey. Three years later, Robert left A.M. Best and joined Skandia Insurance Company, in New York City. The Alexanders subsequently relocated to Warren, shortening Robert's commute by approximately twenty miles. In 1985, Robert accepted a position with the Guy Carpenter division of Marsh & McLennon and moved to an office on the 54th floor of the World Trade Center. When he retired from Guy Carpenter in March of 1995, it is likely that he hadn't the faintest idea that the most productive days of his life were yet to come!

After his retirement, Robert and Gerda made the eminently sensible decision to "downsize." No longer needing access to New York, they made plans to move to a continuing care retirement community in the Pennsylvania countryside west of Harrisburg. They listed their house in New Jersey and contracted to build a new home in the town of Newville. Everything seemed to be moving along well, in accordance with their careful plans.

Then it happened. In June of 1996, Robert received a phone call from his primary care physician reporting that his most recent blood test showed that his prostate specific antigen reading, or PSA,[3] had risen to 20, well above the upper limit of the normal range. The need for an MRI exam was indicated. After two agonizing weeks waiting for a follow-up appointment, Robert and Gerda were to hear a confirmed diagnosis of prostate cancer. Even worse, the cancer had already progressed beyond the prostate gland and was therefore inoperable. Robert was told that he had just fourteen months to live.

One of Robert and Gerda's first actions was to share the diagnosis with the administrators of the continuing care retirement community where they had planned to move. They were concerned that their application might be rejected as a result. But it was not.

When Robert shared his diagnosis with me, I tried to imagine how I would have reacted. His case had been questionably handled by his primary physician. His PSA reading the prior year had risen enough to be cause for concern, and at that time surgery would have been a viable option. In our litigious society, someone else in Robert's shoes might have pursued legal redress, with a good chance for a substantial judgment.

Instead, Robert plunged into research about his disease. Since he wasn't a candidate for either external beam radiation or a radical prostatectomy (surgery to remove the prostate gland), he sought to learn about alternative therapies. He went to the library, searched web sites and read biographies by famous prostate cancer survivors, including Michael Korda, the famed editor and author, and Andrew Grove, one of the founders of Intel. It wasn't long before he was an authority! While his urologist initiated hormonal therapy as a "palliative," Robert took action to augment his immune system through significant dietary and lifestyle changes. Gerda participated every step of the way.

Even before he moved, Robert contacted the Harrisburg office of the American Cancer Society (ACS). Unlike most men they heard from, Robert was not asking for information. He was asking how he could make himself useful! An office worker commented, "You're a Godsend!", followed quickly by, "Would you become a leader?" When Robert responded that he would, he was put in touch with Scott Warrick, another prostate cancer survivor who lived in nearby Harrisburg. When they first met, Scott had some reservations. He recalls:

> "My first impression of Robert…was that he was a somewhat detached, introverted man with little or no warmth and no sense of humor. That impression evaporated over the ensuing years during which he became a colleague, a very close friend, a brother – indeed a man whom I came to admire, respect and love."

Shortly after their initial meeting, Robert became the co-founder, with Scott, and the first facilitator of a Man to Man chapter – an ACS prostate cancer support group in Mechanicsburg. He also served on ACS' cancer control steering committee and traveled throughout the state, training ACS volunteers about prostate cancer awareness.

When he learned that the Hershey Medical Center hosted a chapter of US TOO!, another prostate cancer support group, Robert contacted its leader, Jim Williams. Jim is a decorated career Army officer whose prostate cancer was caught early. He underwent a successful prostatectomy and, since his retirement from the Army, has enjoyed a productive second career as a human resources administrator. When I asked Jim to describe his first impressions of Robert, they mirrored both Scott's and my own from several years earlier: reserved, thoughtful, serious. Still, these men hit it off very quickly, no doubt because they shared a common mission. And with time, as their friendship deepened, Robert's veneer wore away.

In the midst of this newfound activity, Robert perceived a serious problem. Finding a cure required research, and prostate cancer research was woefully underfunded. He attributed this to a lack of awareness, which in turn resulted in insufficient political clout. And the problem was exacerbated by men's innate reluctance to discuss it. Women were miles ahead with their Race for the Cure of breast cancer.

As a first step toward solving this problem, Robert decided he could have an impact in his own back yard. After all, his new home was a relatively short distance from Harrisburg, the state capital. Legislators should be relatively accessible. For maximum impact, he believed that all the disparate prostate cancer support groups in Pennsylvania needed to unite and speak with a single loud voice. With active support from Jim Williams, he founded the Pennsylvania Prostate Cancer Coalition, an umbrella organization that would pool the resources of prostate cancer support groups throughout the state and strengthen their advocacy efforts. He took on the added responsibility of being editor and publisher of the Coalition's newsletter, *Connexions.*

Robert's activities did not go unnoticed. The Department of Defense selected him to sit on their scientific prostate cancer peer review committee, and he was chosen by the National Cancer Institute to assist them as a consumer advocate advisor. He traveled across the country, attending and participating in prostate cancer conferences. And he lobbied both in Harrisburg and in Washington, DC, seeking the additional funding needed for prostate cancer research.

Concurrent with all of these volunteer activities, Robert and Gerda continued to pursue alternative therapies for his disease. They selflessly shared their knowledge with others who were similarly afflicted. Robert maintained faithful e-mail correspondence with a growing list of men whom he was reaching with his ministry. He also purchased and became adept with software which allowed him to produce and send customized greeting cards, often containing inspirational words of encouragement.

At the same time, Robert was growing spiritually. He and Gerda had not yet joined a church in their new community in Pennsylvania, but they were actively looking. In July of 1998, Robert was invited to attend a Promise Keepers gathering at Veterans Stadium in Philadelphia. Although he was already a committed Christian, he later described how the Holy Spirit grabbed hold of him forcefully at that event. His closest friends also noticed a profound change in him, and the Holy Spirit's guidance is clear in his writings from that day forward.

Upon returning from Philadelphia, and to fulfill one of his promises as a Promise Keeper, Robert sought to get involved again in a local men's group. A short time later, he received a call from Jim Small, a cabinetmaker in the neighboring town of Shippensburg. Jim had been to the same Promise Keepers event and learned of Robert's attendance from his pastor. He invited Robert to participate in a weekly Thursday morning study in his shop and recalls that Robert was flabbergasted by this direct and almost immediate answer to his prayer! I believe that, apart from Gerda, Jim was to develop the closest relationship of anyone with Robert during the last years of his life.

Jim has an amusing recollection of their first encounter. His pastor had told him about "Bob" Alexander, and Jim addressed him that way, only to receive the response, in a soft but firm tone, "It's Robert." Over the next two and a half years, Jim heard Robert correct people in that way "hundreds of times." One of his prayers was that Robert would live long enough to stop doing it, but it didn't happen. It was only recently that I learned the origin of this habit from Robert's sister Bonnie. When he was a young child, his immediate family called him Bobby. Upon hearing this during one of her visits, his maternal grandmother intoned, "His name is Robert!" He adopted her insistence from that day forward.

Chapter 3: "Jesus I Love You" (Psalm 1)

"When they had finished eating, Jesus said to Simon Peter, 'Simon, son of John, do you truly love me more than these?' 'Yes, Lord' he said, 'you know that I love you.'" John 21:15 (NIV)

On the weekend of July 10-11, 1998, Robert Alexander attended a Promise Keepers gathering at Veterans Stadium in Philadelphia. By all accounts, it marked a significant turning point in his life. In a letter written two weeks later to Rev. Bill Beck, the pastor at Big Spring Presbyterian Church in Newville, he observed:

> "There was an indescribable fire in the air, a spiritual charge I actually felt throughout my body. That first evening, when John Guest...preached on the theme of commitment and 'coming home to God,' there was a palpable sense of the Holy Spirit's presence, urging me to be among those going forward. As we sang 'Grace Alone,' the brother next to me and I joined hundreds of others streaming from the stands to center field.
>
> "I realized I was indeed face to face with the Lord in that big outdoor tabernacle. An anticipation I hadn't felt in years came over me. It was at that moment I knew the Risen Christ wanted not just me, or my cancer, or my stored up resentments or my repressed anger of back years, or my fears about my family and

myself, *but all of it – my whole life, if only I would yield and give it to Him and recommit myself to faith.* Kneeling on the turf, I silently whispered, 'Lord, I need You now more than ever and I freely offer everything I am to you!'

"On Saturday the messages, prayers and songs underscored for me the solemn commitment I had made Friday night and imbued in me a powerful sense of release from all the tired emotional burdens of the past. I was of all persons most jubilant!

"In the week following I prayed that God would lead me into the company of some other godly men for prayer and fellowship. It must have been an answer to prayer that Jim Small called me one day last week....He invited me to join the small group of men who meet in his cabinetmaking shop each Thursday at 6 a.m. I went ....Seven of us were together for a time of simply studying the Word, talking candidly about our hopes and fears, and praying for and with each other for our daily walk. When 7 o'clock came and we were ready to part, there were bear hugs all around. What a blessing!"

In closing, Robert commented, "This is the hymn that meant so much to me at Promise Keepers:"

Grace Alone[4]

Every promise we can make
Every prayer and step of faith

Every difference we can make
Is only by His grace.

Every mountain we will climb
Every ray of hope we shine
Every blessing left behind
Is only by His grace.

(chorus)
Grace alone
Which God supplies
Strength unknown
He will provide
Christ in us
Our Cornerstone
We will go forth in grace alone.

Every soul we long to reach
Every heart we hope to teach
Everywhere we share His peace
Is only by His grace.

Every loving word we say
Every tear we wipe away
Every sorrow turned to praise
Is only by His grace.

That same month, as best I have been able to determine, Robert wrote his first Psalm. I found it in one of the cards he had made. The card included – and was obviously inspired by – this verse from Scripture:

> *"May the God of peace, who through the blood of the eternal covenant brought back from the dead our Lord Jesus, that great Shepherd of the sheep, equip you with everything good for doing His will, and may He work in us what is pleasing to Him, through Jesus Christ, to whom be glory for ever and ever. Amen."* Hebrews 13:20-21 (NIV)

On the left side of the opened card, Robert expressed his own personal covenant:

I worship Jesus Christ as Alpha and Omega—
the Beginning and the End—for He precedes all and
exceeds all that has or ever shall be.
I receive and acknowledge Him as Saviour and Redeemer,
for He alone is able to provide release and salvation
for me and for mankind.
I honor Him as Lord above all, according to the
Father's desire that every knee bow and every tongue
confess
His name with praise and thanksgiving!
I surrender to His command all that I have and am.
I covenant by His grace to pursue vital relationships
with a few other godly men for the purpose
of encouraging one another toward
love and good deeds.

And I will seek always to be a witness in word and deed
to the love, forgiveness and hope that is given me
Through Christ Jesus my Lord.

—ROBERT HAROLD ALEXANDER
NEWVILLE, PENSYLVANIA
JULY 1998

The words of the psalm itself reflect the sensitivity and awareness of beauty and detail which his sister Bonnie recalled from their youth. Robert was obviously still living the mountaintop experience from his participation with Promise Keepers earlier in the month.

Psalm 1. Jesus I Love You

I love you more than ever
and more than I can say.

I love you when I let my fingers
run along the bark of a birch
feeling the strength and life.

And when in the mornings
I raise the shades
and see the mist rising on the mountain.

When I see a bee
disappearing into the calyx of a flower.

I love you when the setting sun
dips me in blood
and when the fir snaps in
a fierce storm.
I love you when the pebble skips
on the water and doesn't want to sink.
I love you for all the failures in my life
which drove me into your arms,
for the loss of my mind
in order to win your wisdom.

I praise you for all that was
incomprehensible
which caused me fear
and showed me the
vulnerability of my life.

I praise you for all the surprises
which have shaken me up
and opened a new world for me.

I thank you for your nearness,
which fills my life with joy
even when I feel alone and
at the mercy of fear.

Thank you, Jesus—
my Friend....
my Saviour and Redeemer....
my Lord....
my God!

Chapter 4: "Teach Me About Thy Cross, Dear Lord" (Psalm 2)

> *"...Let us run with perseverance the race marked out for us. Let us fix our eyes on Jesus, the author and perfecter of our faith, who for the joy set before him endured the cross..."* Hebrews 12:1-2 (NIV)

True to form, Robert meticulously documented both his condition and his treatment plans. Following his initial diagnosis in the summer of 1996, when his PSA had risen to 40.5, his oncologist in New Jersey initiated monthly monohormonal therapy in August with injections of Lupron, an LHRH agonist.[5] In the course of her own research, Gerda had learned of the Creative Health Institute in Union City, Michigan, where patients could bolster their immune systems by undertaking some significant lifestyle changes. Firmly engaged in this new battle alongside her husband, she insisted that Robert go there as soon as possible. Despite the fact that they had just put their New Jersey home on the market, he acquiesced and spent nearly three weeks there, from September 19 through October 7. His new regimen included an essentially vegetarian diet, with no meats, sugars or caffeine; a cleansing fast; a weight reduction program; and an exercise and walking program.

These actions resulted in a precipitous reduction in his PSA readings. By November it had dropped to 7.7, and Robert and Gerda had every reason to be encouraged. After relocating to Pennsylvania that month, Robert began seeing Dr. R. Scott Owens of Mid Penn Urology in Camp Hill as his specialist. Dr. Owens continued the Lupron injections and supplemented them with daily doses of Casodex, another hormone. Robert's PSA continued a slow, steady decline to a low of 3.7 by December of the following year. However, a reading of 5.7 in March of 1998 showed that it had begun to increase. By August it had jumped to 14.3, prompting Dr. Owens to discontinue the Casodex prescription and to order bone and CT scans. These were done on September 9 and showed "no indication of bone lesions or ambiguities." Through all of this, Robert's faith appeared to be growing. He felt enriched by his small men's group, which he referred to as "our Blue Mountain fellowship," and particularly blessed by his friendship with Jim Small.. In mid-September, Gerda flew to Germany to visit her brothers and sisters. Robert made arrangements to follow her, but only after first participating in a March on Cancer on September 26 in Washington. On the previous Sunday evening, he had invited Jim to his home, to talk and to enjoy some of the healthy food which Gerda had prepared before her departure. After Jim's visit, Robert sent a card to his friend. I have excerpted from it, with Jim's permission:

> "Dear Jim,
>
> "....In the quiet of the cottage, I've been musing over our special time together late this afternoon and evening....I thank you for listening to some more of my story. Now, as I reflect on it, I certainly hope I didn't monopolize the conversation. Surely there were many things you wished to say, too!...
>
> "Doesn't the Holy Spirit have a gentle yet pointed way of dealing with each of us?

> Lessons from God's Eternal Word serve as a strong warning as well as a comforting assurance to me: If I keep my heart humble before the Lord, I can be certain of His highest purposes being realized in my life. That's the kind of heart I really want. Always. I pray that may be so for you also....Thank you for your prayers for me and the meeting last Thursday.
>
> "I just now stopped and re-read Chambers[6] for September 20, 'The Divine Rule of Life.' The Scripture verse is Matthew 5:48. His comments hit home: 'The expression of Christian character is not good doing, but God-likeness....God's life in us expresses itself as God's life, not as human life trying to be godly.'
>
> "Chambers says the secret of a Christian life is that the supernatural is made natural in him by the grace of God....and what's more amazing, that 'the experience of this works out in the practical details of life, not in times of communion with God.' Jim, sometimes I have to pinch myself: God is allowing me to actually live NOW as a Resurrection Person....that life can be and is really this great! (Oh, the struggles we have with self-doubts!)"

Under the heading, "A Cautionary Thought," Robert added these words:

"I read that most believers face a hurdle called 'romanticism' in the course of their growth in the Lord Jesus. You and I must find a way to leap that hurdle…or be tripped up again and again. I don't mean a deeply emotional or sentimental feeling toward our Lord is wrong. It isn't. Such feelings should never be lost. But we can not depend on them alone. We need to go deeper. As I write these words, I think of the words to the PK[7] song, 'Knowing You (All I Once Held Dear).' Doesn't it conclude with 'You're the best…You're my righteousness…and I love you, Lord'?"

Three days later, on the evening of September 23, Robert sent another card to Jim, after they had attended a Bible study at the Big Spring Presbyterian Church in Newville. What is particularly striking is that Robert, who throughout his life had had relatively superficial relationships with most acquaintances, had become so open and vulnerable with his new friend, someone he had known for less than two months.

"Dear Jim,

"Thank you for your prayers for me….After tonight's Bible study, when I came home, I went back and re-read Oswald Chambers[8] for July 23, 'Sanctification.' The Scripture verse is I Cor. 1:30. He says the mystery of sanctification is 'that the perfections of Jesus

Christ are imparted to me, not gradually, but instantly when by faith I enter into the realization that Jesus Christ is made unto me sanctification.' Chambers goes on to say, 'Sanctification does not mean anything less than the holiness of Jesus being made mine manifestly.' I think I understand that statement. And, of course, I believe it's His wonderful life that is imparted to us by faith as a sovereign gift of God's grace.

"Chambers uses the word 'impartation' when he talks about our receiving the holy qualities of the Lord Jesus Christ (i.e., His patience, His love, His holiness, His faith, His purity, His godliness). I'd fall flat on my face if I were to try this by imitation! But, if it's an instantaneous gift, Chambers still points out that while all the perfections of Jesus are at my disposal, it's 'slowly and surely [that] I begin to live a life of ineffable order and sanity and holiness: Kept by the power of God.'

"Some time perhaps you and I can talk a bit more about sanctification?....I would confess to you that for some reason tonight at the Bible Study I began to feel 'less than.' I don't know quite why, but maybe it was seeing all those GRV[9] faces (which ought not to spook me, I admit)....

"Allow me to switch to the neat discovery I told you about the other day on the phone. It was the passage in Genesis (Gen. 13:17), where the Lord tells Abram to *walk* through the land He had shown him, that would be his and his descendants'. It wasn't just *seeing* it, but relishing each acre of His gift, claiming what God had promised as true.

"It struck me that the same is true for the Christian life. When we read through the Gospels we are amazed by what our Lord has told He would do for us. He promised an abundant life now and an eternal life forever. All power would be given to us. He would be with us. Our hearts would become His home. [That's from whence came the 'indwelling Christ' within us that I mentioned tonight.] As with Abram, walking through the promise God had made, I believe to claim what Christ has offered is our challenge. Otherwise we live as spiritual paupers when unlimited resources are placed at our disposal! As I write these words with such conviction, I also sense a certain weakness in myself, causing me to desire the Holy Spirit so to embrace me that I won't get caught in those moments of faintheartedness. Perhaps it's simply my failure/weakness to appropriate the promises the Lord has made. How strong and courageous in the Lord we can feel some days, and, yet on other days, pretty feeble. My comfort is that He created me, knows me in my most inward parts, and holds me in the palm of His hand – always!

"As I share this with you, I remember our PK promises, that men need to be able to share such inmost thoughts with their brothers. I just lift you up for the blessing you've been to me....

"It's getting late, my dear friend and brother. I must sign off now. I thank you for being such a blessing in my life, Jim! God bless you. Much love to you in Christ. I pray for you always. Robert"

After participating in the March on Cancer in Washington on the 26th, Robert flew to Hannover, Germany on the 28th to join Gerda and her family. They returned to Pennsylvania in mid-October, with Robert now sporting a professorial gray beard. They had also received somewhat encouraging news on the medical front — that Robert's most recent PSA, taken before his departure, had dropped to 12.1.

It was about this time that Robert appears to have written his second psalm. I found it on a card to his Thursday morning fellowship group, dated October 19. Robert's cards often contained a verse from a favorite hymn on the front, and he was careful to make attribution to the author. This card contained a verse, too, but with no such attribution. After careful and fairly extensive research, I have concluded that Robert authored it himself, and I have therefore incorporated it into what I have called his second psalm.

Psalm 2. "Teach Me About Thy Cross, Dear Lord"

Teach me about Thy Cross, dear Lord,
nothing presumed, I've all to learn.

Spirit of God, unfold the Word;
Thy deepest secrets let me learn.
Prone to indulge my selfish whims;
failing to learn Thy purity.
Bent on my will, my pride, my sins;
teach of Thy Cross and liberate me.
Make of Thy Cross a yoke for me;
crowd me toward life,
all sin erase.
Discipline every energy;
Lord, may Thy glory
illuminate my face.

An amazing truth!

From the moment of my entry into
the saving life
Jesus has given me by His death on the
Cross, through a lifetime of learning to walk
in His love and power,
it's all grace!

He gives it.
Nothing is earned.
Nothing is actuated
by my strength or power.

So, Lord, I pray, let flow forth fresh
watercourses of Holy Spirit fullness
and power in my life.
Let the flow bear me forward. I don't want
to become a stagnant pool of former blessing,
but a rising river of
fresh inspiration.

And, Lord, I pray, let the rivers run deep.
I don't want to be shallow
in any part of my life.
Let the sandbars of carnal obstruction in my
nature be furrowed out by the force of
this stream of living waters.
And, Lord, let me learn to flow together with
other believers,
as streams become tributaries
to a larger river.
Let any smallness or mean spiritedness
become lost in my surrender
to Your Spirit's blending me with all
those who love You in truth.
Let me move with them in the
grace and power of Jesus' life and love.
Come, Holy Spirit....
as rivers of living water
for me and my brothers in Christ.

I would ask that you lift up in your prayers
two members of my cancer support group
(Harold and Joe) - praying
for their comfort and peace.
Both men are living with
metastatic bone pain from prostate cancer.

To David and Jim and each brother in our
Thursday fellowship group,
I pray for you always.
God's grace.

Robert
OCTOBER 19, 1998

Chapter 5: "At Autumn: A Prayer for Jim" (Psalm 3)

> *"[For my determined purpose is] that I may know Him – that I may progressively become more deeply and intimately acquainted with Him, perceiving and recognizing and understanding [the wonders of His Person] more strongly and more clearly. And that I may in that same way come to know the power outflowing from His resurrection [which it exerts over believers]; and that I may so share in His sufferings as to be continually transformed [in spirit unto His likeness even] to His death."* Philippians 3:10 (Amplified New Testament)

Robert's bonds with his Thursday morning "Blue Mountain Fellowship," and particularly with Jim Small, continued to strengthen. While Robert and Jim became brothers immediately – Robert was soon to begin calling Jim his Jonathan – Jim observed, with some bemusement, how quickly Robert was assimilated into the rest of the group. Jim describes them as representing "the entire cultural spectrum," including drywall finishers and laborers, as well as recovering alcoholics and drug addicts, now reborn. On returning for his second week, Robert had adapted his dress to conform!

On October 22, 1998, Robert sent the group one of his trademark cards. The cover contained the Amplified New Testament translation of Philippians 3:10. The contents inside indicated that this had been Robert's chosen life verse, as it had clearly affected the path his life had followed:

"To Jim and my dear brothers in Christ—

"Thank you for giving me the copy of the prayer you wrote several years ago but had not shown to anyone else. I treasure having a copy for myself. Photocopies of it have been made as you requested. These were reproduced on good laid paper (together with two copies done on my computer), suitable for framing as you wish. You'll recall I felt the beginning paragraph tied in with the balance of the text – and so I left it that way. Now, as I re-read it, the words speak to similar conditions in my life. I feel convicted of precisely those very same things – and, truthfully, probably more.

"In my delight to discover you as a brother in Christ, I acknowledge having expected too much of your time and attention. Only our Lord Jesus Christ can rightfully claim full allegiance of our hearts and minds. As Oswald Chambers[10] points out, 'Our Lord knows that every relationship not based on [total] loyalty to Himself will end in disaster.' I am beginning to understand why 'our Lord Jesus Christ trusted no man, yet He was never suspicious, never bitter.' The lesson for me, as I progress along the Calvary Road, is to realize that form of disillusionment – which comes from God – brings me to the place where I can see men and women as they really are – no more grand illusions, unfulfilled expectations or aching disappointments. Further, I now also know that, when my fealty rests in the Lord, there will be no cynicism, no stinging, bitter thoughts, no agony of despair, no feelings of rejection or of lack of worth. I am discovering anew there is only one Being Who can satisfy the last aching abyss of the human heart, and that is the Lord Jesus Christ!

"Let me do a flashback to the time of the Korean War in the early 50's:

"I remember well an earlier turning point in my life as a young Marine, traveling back to my ship at the Norfolk naval base from weekend liberty. I was sitting in the back seat of a busload of snoring sailors, thumbing through my new copy of the Amplified New Testament with the aid of a flashlight. There that verse was, waiting to be discovered....to be believed....to be put into action. *Philippians 3:10 said all I needed to hear*:

"I heard it then and it changed me, my service career, and my choice in education. Afterwards, during the intervening years of college, family and career, I indeed wandered at times away from my Lord. And yet, though it took decades for that Philippians 3:10 seed to finally sprout, it sprang up at another turning point this summer when I recommitted my life to Christ at Promise Keepers in Philadelphia! It was then that I remembered the passage afresh: 'That's it....that's *everything* in one grand statement!'

"I don't believe our Lord wastes times of testing. The pains and struggles and confusion connected with my circumstances only *seemed* futile and unfair. His Word holds out hope when all else seems hopeless.

"Now I feel impelled to know Him better. I was struck by the lyrics to PK's song, *'Knowing You (All I Once Held Dear)'*[11]:

All I once held dear, built my life upon,
All this world reveres and wars to own.
All I once thought gain I have counted loss,
spent and worthless now
Compared to this:
Knowing You, Jesus, knowing You,
There is no greater thing.
You're my all, You're the best, You're my joy,
My righteousness, and I love You, Lord.
And I love You, Lord.

"I desire now to model the power outflowing from His resurrection. And I want to be continually transformed into His likeness....which I believe requires accepting my share of suffering through a Gethsemane experience....it means a conscious choice leading to the agony of brokenness and yieldedness....receiving the healing that will take away even my greatest shame...and, finally, becoming dead to self. As I petition the Lord at this time to give me someone who will help me bear the burden of the Cross and this

> death, I'd like to be absolutely transparent with you and those around me in this most critical matter. May God grant me a fellow believer to assist me through this period (James 5:16).
>
> "Jim, I pray always for you and my brothers in Christ. By God's grace,
>
> Robert
>
> October 22, 1998"

At the bottom of the card, Robert added:

> "We cannot see the way God is going to work where we are right now, but I am sure he does: *'For the mountains shall depart and the hills be removed, but My kindness shall not depart from you, nor shall My covenant of peace be removed, says the Lord, Who has mercy on you.' (Isaiah 54:10)."*

A day later, Robert sent a personal message to Jim. It was beautifully formatted, almost like a newsletter, and covered a variety of topics. It began:

> *"We rejoice, Jim, because we are rightly related to Jesus...(Luke 10:19, 20).* Thank you for your most welcome letter of October 20 with the addresses for both Tom and Kent. Your letters always please me because you can be so expressive, you include such apt Bible references, and, not least, there are always some artistic and humorous touches. It is a

delight to my mind and soul to receive such writings....

"Now I've got to get down to work, and studying the eight grant applications I've been assigned to critique at the NCI panel on November 5-6. Since this commitment follows in the wake of an ACS seminar November 1-3 in Atlanta, I need to be careful about my time so I do those things and yet don't dishonor my promises to my lovely Gerda.

"Your thought was most appreciated about adding 2 Peter 1:3-9 to the 1 Peter reading I had mentioned to you. You're right: Nothing quite comforts, assures and empowers like those passages! I have displayed the full text of these verses (at left and right) to gain a better appreciation of them. This is both an exercise in typography for me as well as affording one time to physically 'work with' and 'absorb' the Word.

"It was also thoughtful for you to write, 'I pray for us, Hebrews 12:1-2.' And, as I now engage in prayer for us with the words from those verses, I have added verses 14-15, which contain the admonition to us to see 'that *no bitter root* grows up to cause trouble and defile many.' You'll note the focus on bitter roots (as in strongholds), which to me seems to be quite appropriate, don't you agree?

"In James we read, '*Don't be deceived, my dear brothers. Every good and perfect gift is from above, coming down from the Father of the heavenly lights, Who does not change like shifting shadows. He chose to give us birth through the word of truth, that we might be a kind of first fruits of all He created.' (James 1:16-18). Jim, I love you and I pray for you and for David always.*

By God's grace, your brother in Christ,

Robert"

In another card to the group, composed on October 28, Robert reflected again on God's awesome grace. He titled it, "A Message for Us Misfits:"

"Chuck Swindoll has thoughtfully dug into Judges 11 and 12 to focus on the story of Jephthah. Before he ever came to the plate, Jephthah had three strikes against him. He was an illegitimate child. ***Strike One***. He was the son of a barmaid and a brute. ***Strike Two***. He was raised in an atmosphere of hatred and hostility. ***Strike Three***.

"Judges 11:6,8 recounts how the Israelites, faced with possible humiliation at the hands of the Ammonites, called on Jephthah, the hoodlum, to be their chief in annihilating the foe. And that chore he did! What a switch for Jephthah to become the Judge over Israel! He had no right to such a high calling. This would have been true except for one thing: **God's grace**. Remember now, God is the one who builds trophies from the scrap pile....who draws His clay from under the bridge....who makes clean instruments of beauty from the filthy human failures of yesterday. To underscore this truth, we ought to consider Paul's stunning remark made to a group of unsophisticated Corinthian Christians:

'Do not be deceived: Neither the sexually immoral nor idolaters nor adulterers nor male prostitutes nor homosexual offenders nor thieves nor the greedy nor drunkards nor slanderers nor swindlers will inherit the kingdom of God. And that is what some of you were.' (1 Cor. 6:9-11 NIV)

"We dare not rush over those last eight words: '***And that is what some of you [us] were.***'

"God our Father, in great grace loved us when you and I were Jephthah – a rebel or a drunk or a gossip or a crook or a liar or a brawler or a Pharisee or a playboy or an adulterer or a hypocrite or a do-gooder or a back-slider or a drop-out or a drug addict or a malcontent. Looking for sinners, He found us in our desperate straits. Lifting us to the level of His much-loved Son, he brought us in, washed and healed our wounds, and changed our direction. **Praise God!**

"All our church-going and hymn-singing and long-praying and committee-sitting and religious-talking will never ease the fact that we were dug from a deep, dark, deadly pit. And may we never forget it! Classic misfits....we. But there is one major difference between Jephthah and us. God chose to reveal his past for everyone to read, while He chose to hide ours so hardly anyone would ever know what colossal misfits we really are. **Now that's GRACE!**

"As we think of God's marvelous **grace** to us, let us remember it is *we* who have hauled the cross out of sight. It is *we* who have left the impression that it belongs only in the cloistered halls of a seminary or beneath the soft shadows of stained glass and marble statues. This piece, written by George MacLeod, of Scotland's Iona community, convicts my spirit:

'I simply argue that the cross be raised again at the center of the market place as well as on the steeple of the church. I am recovering the claim that Jesus was not crucified in a cathedral between two candles, but on a cross between two thieves; on a town garbage heap; at a crossroad of politics so cosmopolitan that they had to write His title in Hebrew and in Latin and in Greek....and at the kind of place where cynics talk smut, and thieves curse and soldiers gamble. Because that is where He died, and that is what He died about. And that is where Christ's men ought to be, and what church people ought to be about.'

"May this touch your spirit, too. I pray always for you and each brother-in-Christ in our Thursday morning fellowship.

By God's grace,

Robert

October 28, 1998"

As he had indicated in his earlier card to Jim, Robert traveled to Atlanta for four days of training with the American Cancer Society, from November 1-4. This afforded Jim and Gerda a unique opportunity. Fred Hachmeister, his college roommate, had recalled that Robert could never throw anything away! As a voracious reader, prolific writer, college class president, prostate cancer researcher/activist.....he had literally filled his and Gerda's garage with paper and files! He recognized this was a problem and had given Gerda his blessing to dispose of most of it, save for a few cherished items...*if* she could find them! But Gerda, knowing how much his research had meant to him, could never bring herself to do it. Robert had then implored Jim and asked, "What do I need to do to have you help Gerda?" In jest, Jim had replied, "Get down on your knees and beg!" And Robert did just that!

At the time, Jim had a farm in a county where open burning was permitted. He also had a pick-up truck. So while Robert was away in Atlanta – she couldn't dare to do it in his presence! – Gerda worked diligently, past midnight, sorting through boxes. Then, with Jim, she filled his truck. They were unable to complete the job, but they had made a sizable dent. Jim recalls that the fire burned for several days!

Upon his return from Atlanta, Robert proceeded immediately to critique grant applications at an NCI panel on the 5th and 6th. Four days later, he sent a card to Jim Small, with the simple caption, *"A prayer for Jim from Robert."* It contained Robert's third psalm, which again reflected Robert's sensitivity and profound appreciation for the beauty of God's creation.

Psalm 3. At Autumn

All this splendor, God surrounds me,
I cannot contain it all.
Gifts abound by your hand given,
Seen in great things and in small,
Tow'ring mountains to witness
Of my Creator's skill,
While a baby's touch is speaking
Of my loving Father's will.

What high and special praise we
give to our blessed Lord God,
the Creator of earth's beauty. Nothing
can dull our senses to the magnificence
He shines usward -
especially at season-changes.
May you rejoice with me, and while noting
the grandeur of His creative working,
take comfort in the personal and
tender touch of His hand toward

you and me.

Praise is an atmosphere through which
the Adversary cannot move.
As we enter into this truth,
it will transform our lives.
And it's not, I believe, simply
because praise can insulate us
or protect us.
It's got to be more than that!
It's because He is worthy....
worthy of the best of our praise,
the depth of our thanksgiving
for His Grace!

Father God, as we therefore offer You our
ongoing and unbounded praise, I would ask,

"Come, Holy Spirit....as rivers of
living water and the pure Fountain of Grace,
for me and my brothers in Christ."

Jim, I pray for you always,
and for David also.

Much love in Christ—

Robert

November 10, 1998

Robert closed the card with these verses:

"May the God of peace, Who through the blood of the eternal covenant brought back from the dead our Lord Jesus, that great Shepherd of the sheep, equip you with everything good for doing His will, and may He work in us what is pleasing to Him, through Jesus Christ, to whom be glory forever and ever. Amen." Hebrews 13:20-21(NIV)

Chapter 6: "Sing Me to Heaven" (Psalm 4)

"He said unto me, 'Son of man, stand up on your feet and I will speak to you.' As he spoke, the Spirit came into me and raised me to my feet, and I heard him speaking to me." Ezekiel 2:1-2 (NIV)

Robert continued to devour God's Word. With every new revelation, he seemed to almost burst in sharing it. I found one example in a card he sent to Jim Small on November 16, 1998, where he reflected on the meaning of love. The cover again contained his life verse, Philippians 3:10, then:

"Dear Jim,

"I just want to share with you the exciting discovery I made today in our devotionals when Gerda and I were studying 1 Cor. 12! You'll recall that this is where Paul tells the believers at Corinth that the qualities of life for which they [and, by inference, we] long most are really not humanly produced. They are divinely imputed! Wow! Paul helpfully lists the gifts of the Spirit and says these do come to us through the operation of the Holy Spirit. I went back over this list. The greatest gift of all – love – is missing. Did he forget? No, it is held for us to read in Chapter 13. And there Paul clarifies for me what is meant by love. Furthermore, what he is saying is that most importantly, love is a gift. This concept eluded me for a long time. I can receive love and I can be a communicator or bearer of it, but, in and of myself, *I cannot produce it!*

"It struck me powerfully what this means: I cannot love in *a giving, forgiving, free, unmotivated, unchanging, uncalculating way* until the gift is given to me. Hence, all my earlier efforts to really love others apart from God's power have been self-centered and selective – even when I felt or thought I was truly being Unconditional! (A terrible but real fact!)

"So now (as a Child once again), I am relearning that the Holy Spirit is LOVE, and when He lives in us, we are able to love because He loves through us.

"Then I noted how Paul takes all the honored human qualities and exposes them one by one as inadequate unless we have received the gift of love. (I must have heard all this years before, but wasn't attuned to it, I must say!) Paul sets the qualities up and makes them march before our mind's eye as what I'd call a 'cadre of devaluated causes.'

"I believe Paul is telling me that these causes are absolutely worthless if the *gift of love* is lacking. Neither *eloquence, nor prophecy, nor absolute faith*, can compare with *love*.

"Even the power to do miraculous things is nothing if we lack the power to love another person as God loves us. *'This is love, not that we loved God but that He loved us and sent His son to be an atoning sacrifice for our sins.'* (1 John 4:10)

"Moreover, I now have a better grasp of why God sent the Holy Spirit to indwell in us and enable us to convey that love to other Christians. I believe I now understand what it means to be able to say to you with all the sincerity I possess, that I love you as a brother in Christ – yet it is not I, but the power of Christ dwelling within me. All praise be to the Lord for this discovery!

"Jim, I pray always for you, for the brothers in our Thursday fellowship group, and for David.

By God's grace,
Robert
November 16, 1998"

At the bottom of the card, Robert closed by adding this personalized verse:

> *"Let the word of Christ dwell in [us] richly as [we] teach and admonish one another with all wisdom, and as [we] sing psalms, hymns, and spiritual songs with gratitude in [our] hearts to God. And whatever [we] do, whether in word or deed, [may we] do it all in the name of the Lord Jesus, giving thanks to God the Father through Him."* (Col. 3:17)

On November 30, 1998, Robert's PSA reading showed a pronounced jump, to 16.9. Two days later, on December 2, his records show that "Dr. Owens commenced Triple Blockade Hormonal Therapy, [consisting of] 3-month Lupron injections, plus Eulexin (2 capsules, 125 mg, every 8 hours) and Proscar (1 dose, 5 mg, a.m and p.m.)" This massive regimen was not without side effects. Robert commented about them on December 4 in a message to Kent Fry, a member of his beloved Blue Mountain fellowship who had apparently missed their latest get-together:

> "Dear Kent,
>
> "I just praise God for the prayer time Jim and Howard and I had on Thursday morning! It lifted me beyond the temporary nausea of these two new 'blockbuster' medications. The enclosed prayer is based on some of what was in our prayers on Thursday. It's difficult to remember all the words that the Spirit gave us, but it was such a powerful, uplifting time for me as I believe it was for Howard and Jim, too.
>
> "Today I seem to be tolerating the new chemotherapeutics much better. Still impotent physically in a certain sense, but 'empowered' and fit nonetheless for the Lord's service.
>
> "I pray for you always, Kent, as my brother in Christ, and for each man in our fellowship group.

By God's grace,
Robert
December 4, 1998"

On a number of his cards, Robert began by reproducing an excerpt from a favorite anthem by Daniel Gawthrop,[12] which he titled, "Sing Me to Heaven." It was on the cover of a card he had dated December 4, 1998.

Sing Me to Heaven

In my heart's sequestered chambers lie truths
stripped of poet's gloss. Words alone are vain and
vacant and my heart is mute. In response to
aching silence memory summons half-heard voices,
and my soul finds primal eloquence and wraps me in song.
If you would comfort me, sing me a
lullaby. If you would win my heart, sing me a love song.
If you would mourn me and bring me to God, sing me a
requiem. Sing me to Heaven. Touch in me all love and
passion; pain and pleasure. Touch in me grief and comfort;
love and passion. Sing me a lullaby, a love song, a requiem.
Love me; comfort me; bring me to God.
Sing me a love song.
Sing me to Heaven.

The inner pages of the card were filled with what Robert called, "A prayer with and for Jim and Howard and Robert." I have taken the liberty of appropriating Daniel Gawthrop's title for it and have called it Robert's fourth psalm. Robert conformed to the ACTS acronym (Adoration,

Confession, Thanksgiving and Supplication) in composing it.

Psalm 4. Sing Me to Heaven

O gracious Heavenly Father, because you created us You know us in our most inward parts.

Adoration

As children of Your covenant, we worship You. We lift up and magnify Your name above all names. You are our God and King; our very lives belong to You.

Confession

We acknowledge and confess our weaknesses, our brokenness, our failure to obey Your command to practice purity, our pridefulness, our bent toward sinfulness and willfulness, our failure to forgive others and even to receive forgiveness from You and our fellow men. But, through the blood of Jesus Christ, we are bold to approach Your mercy seat, seeking Your cleansing, Your forgiveness, Your healing.

Thanksgiving

We rejoice that You have called together this fellowship of godly men to worship You and study Your Word. We thank You for the privilege of intercessory prayer for ourselves and our brothers in Christ. We praise You that You alone know our every need before we even ask, that the Holy Spirit gently heals inner hurts and binds up all our wounds.

Supplication

We remember Your words to Ezekiel: "Stand Up, Stand Tall, and Stand Ready!" You got him on his feet, filled him with Your Spirit, and fed him with Your Word. We sense that what You wanted to **do** through Ezekiel, You first did **in** him. So we pray that as you get us on our feet, we will receive Your Holy Spirit. As we feed on Your life-changing Word, may these **words** be engrafted in us. We pray they will give us comfort in our afflictions as well as authority in our witness to others.

Chapter 7: "Te Deum Laudamus" (Psalm 5)

"I will sing to the Lord, for He has been good to me."
Psalm 13:6 (NIV)

During the month of December 1998, Robert wrote another, deeply introspective psalm. It reflects some of the dynamics in his Thursday morning fellowship, and I am indebted to Jim Small for his help in understanding what Robert was going through at the time.

While he had latched on to Jim, as well as the group in general, Robert felt a strong need for acceptance and approval. However, he often failed to express his needs to the point where the others heard. And that would leave him disappointed. He recognized that he had some barriers that he needed to drop. Jim is sure that, in his quiet time with God, God would tell him, "I know" and just put the balm on Robert. And perhaps that's what opened his heart so beautifully as he revealed his innermost thoughts and feelings in his psalms.

Robert attributed the inspiration for this particular psalm to "verses from the pen of Ted Loder, Germantown, Pennsylvania." I have been unable to ascertain Ted Loder's identity, but one of Robert's boyhood homes was in Germantown, so he could have been a family acquaintance.

Psalm 5. Te Deum Laudamus (We Praise You, Lord)

Dearest Jesus,
Deliver me from assuming
Your mercy is gentle.
Pressure me that I may grow more human,
Not through the lessening of my struggles,
But through an expansion of them
That will undamn me
And unbury my gifts.

Deepen my hurt
Until I learn to share it
And myself openly,
And my needs honestly.

Sharpen my fears
Until I name them
And release the power I have locked in them
And they in me.

Accentuate my confusion
Until I shed those grandiose expectations
That divert me from the small, glad gifts
Of the now and the here and the me.

Expose my shame where it shivers,
Crouched behind the curtains of propriety,
Until I can laugh at last
Through my common frailties and failures,
Laugh my way toward becoming
healed and whole.

Deliver me
From just going through the motions
And wasting everything I have
Which is today,
A chance,
A choice,
My creativity,
Your call.

O persistent Jesus,
Let how much it all matters
Pry me off dead center
So if I am moved inside
To tears
Or sighs
Or screams
Or smiles
Or dreams,
They will be real.

And I will more fully understand who
You have created me to be.
And what You, Lord Jesus,
Would have me
Truly become,
As I freely give You the right to my own self.
Te deum laudamus.

Chapter 8: "A New Creation" (Psalm 6)

> *"Therefore, if anyone is in Christ, he is a new creation; the old has gone, the new has come!"* 2 Corinthians 5:17 (NIV)

In their Christmas letter at the end of 1998, Robert and Gerda recounted the highlights of their year. It belied their status as retirees and clearly reflected their joy-filled life.

> "Dear Family and Friends: It has been a time of assurance and spiritual growth for both of us as we've traveled the pathway of faith through cancer survivorship these past two years. We rejoice to share here some highlights of 1998:
>
> "First we should tell you how beautiful it is living out here in Pennsylvania's Cumberland Valley! Our cottage is lovely and our neighbors are the best you could ever want! Early in the year saw the birth of the *Pennsylvania Prostate Cancer Connexion*, a quarterly newsletter Robert and Jim Williams started for all the support group leaders in our state. It was the second year of growth for the Man To Man group Scott Warrick and Robert helped organize in Mechanicsburg, now up to 105 men. In the spring Gerda and Robert again spent two weeks at Creative Health Institute in Michigan, returning to Ann Arbor in late July for the First International Symposium for the Prostate Cancer Patient (along with 1400 other

attendees). Faced with a rising PSA, in September Robert had CT and Bone Scans, which thankfully showed no bone lesions or other ambiguities. We're positive our Whole Foods Diet has a lot to do with the good health we've enjoyed and the immune system response that has been keeping the cancer at bay. During the spring and summer, Robert worked with many other survivors in NPCC advocacy efforts to raise the level of Congressional awareness of the need for substantial funding for prostate cancer research. Starting from scratch, it was a hard fight, but, in the end, we were blessed with a substantial increase in DoD funding as well as an earmarking of research funds for prostate cancer in the National Institutes of Health budget for FY 1999.

"In mid-September Gerda went ahead to Germany to visit her brothers and sisters, with Robert following her to Hannover on Sept. 28, after participating in the March on Cancer Sept. 26 in Washington. We both enjoyed a really special time with Gerda's sisters, Helga and Ruth. Coming home with a gray beard, Robert began a new (for him) Triple Blockade hormonal treatment modality. Our return from Germany was just in time to attend a superb 40th wedding anniversary surprise for Bob and Shirley Weitzel done with aplomb by Patti, Emily and Andrew! Oh yes, lest we forget it, during the winter and spring, Robert was again asked to be an advocate on several NCI scientific review panels….

"In July Robert was invited by men from nearby Green Spring Brethren in Christ Church to attend the Promise Keepers stadium event in Philadelphia (fortunately, stadium railings were no problem then). For our three busloads of men and their sons, this was an extraordinary event. It has meant a transformation in Robert's personal faith and enormous personal growth in our married life together. Two other blessings flowing from that event have been opportunities to participate in a Thursday morning men's fellowship group and to sing in the Newburg Area Men's Chorus. We close on that high note. Rejoice with our warmest good wishes and much love for Christmas. May it be so for you also in the New Year A.D. 1999! GERDA AND ROBERT"

Little more than a week later, I received the New Year's card from Robert that was to become the catalyst for this book. It contained his sixth psalm.

Psalm 6. A New Creation

Glorious God, my Creator and Lord,
This day is all praise and thanks
For all my days.
I breathe and it is Your breath that fills me.

*I look and it is Your light by which I see.
I move and it is Your energy moving in me.
I listen and even the stones speak of You.
I touch and You are between finger and skin.
I think and the thoughts are but sparks
from the fire of Your truth.
I love and the throb is Your presence.
I laugh and it is the rustle of Your passing.
I weep and Your Spirit broods over me.*

*I long and it is the tug of your kingdom.
I praise You,
Glorious Heavenly Father,
For this curious day,
For the impulses that have made it unique
To Gerda and to me,
For the gifts that grace it,
For the gladness that accompanies it.*

*I thank You for all the undeserved blessings
You have given us:
Each special person you have placed
Here in front of us this day,
that we might nurture and
love them in Christ's name,
For the affliction you have given me and the
Comfort wherewith I may comfort those who*

Also are afflicted.

I pause to praise and thank You
With this one more trip of words
Which leaves too much uncarried,
But not unfelt,
Unlived,
Unloved.

Thank you, my dearest Jesus,
My Lord, My God, My All in All!

Your Robert
December 31, 1998

Chapter 9: "Only in You, Lord Jesus" (Psalm 7)

> *"We also rejoice in our sufferings, because we know that suffering produces perseverance; perseverance, character; and character, hope. And hope does not disappoint us, because God has poured out His love into our hearts by the Holy Spirit, whom He has given us."* – Romans 5:3-5 (NIV)

In the fall of 1998, my family relocated to Annapolis. But in January 1999, when I was back in New Jersey on a business trip, I found time one Friday morning to rejoin the Executive Ministries Bible study that I had attended. Since Robert had also participated in that group before moving to Pennsylvania in 1996, I took the opportunity to share the card I had received from him. Also in attendance that day was a man I had not met, Mark Papera. Mark took note of Robert's e-mail address and contacted him a few weeks later. This initiated a correspondence that quickly developed into an in-depth prayer partnership.

Robert was tireless in his advocacy efforts on behalf of men and families afflicted with prostate cancer. At the same time, he recognized that his personal trials with this disease had also yielded some positive dividends. In a talk he delivered at the State Capitol in Harrisburg in January 1999, he reflected on what he described as "the paradigm of prostate cancer" and the profound effect it had had on his and Gerda's lives:

> "Faced with a diagnosis of Stage C prostate cancer, Gerda — I consider her very much a

'prostate cancer survivor,' too! — and I undertook as our personal challenge getting to the root of the problem: To more clearly understand the accepted causes of prostate cancer and all the various treatment options. This was based on the assumption *that such knowledge would enable us to make those positive, radical lifestyle changes in nutrition and diet,* which we came to believe had the potential to significantly improve treatment outcomes for me beyond hormonal or other conventional therapy options.

"At the time of the initial diagnosis, I recalled a brief conversation I had overheard just a few months earlier. Some of my classmates were discussing the trauma of cancer at my fiftieth high school reunion. When someone plainly said, 'Cancer is the best thing that ever happened to me!' those very words almost knocked my socks off! Those few cancer victors, however, were demonstrating ultimate courage by relating how they had each turned adversity into a major victory. It's not the cancer but the positive response to the disease that makes all the difference in the world! Thus the take-home message is, '*Attitude determines outcome.'*

"The following is not an understatement: *Prostate cancer can be a crisis of unparalleled proportions for both the individual and his family, unless something else (read 'radical lifestyle change') happens along with the big wake-up call.* And so, as I came to terms with my own health situation over the next few months, I began to see that in the crisis of my prostate cancer were the seeds of an incredible opportunity, the paradigm of prostate cancer, if you will!

"Do you remember what a paradigm is? The dictionary defines it as an *outstandingly clear or typical example or archetype.* Dr. Stephen B. Strum, well-known oncologist in Culver City, California, writing in *The Prostate Cancer Exchange*, goes further, calling it 'a new way of thinking, a new insight that allows for growth, evolution, and creative initiatives.' Dr. Strum emphasizes that 'Prostate cancer is an important paradigm. It is a blessing to those who see the opportunities that arise out of this life-threatening experience!'

"I can testify that Dr. Strum is right on target, emphasizing that *our response* to this experience can enhance love, generate hope and faith, and it does indeed lead to a peace that may not be experienced without it. Our response to cancer not only can and does create powerful bonds of friendship, it intensifies our enjoyment of all Creation and allows transformation of our souls to new heights of beauty and appreciation. Thus, our response to cancer can lead to a spirit that is beyond our comprehension. We need first only to shed our fear by showing our faith in one another. In giving of ourselves to our neighbors, we enrich our own lives. Put another way, 'In the giving is the getting.'

"As husband and wife survivors, we learned that we could no longer be inner-directed or selfish with our time, our energy, our material things. In my own experience, the giving of our love and energy, in all of its manifestations, has clearly brought about remarkable positive changes in our physical and spiritual health. Now, almost a three-year survivor — whose life expectancy at diagnosis was calibrated at less time — I am grateful for that erroneous calculation. I am impelled to repeat that the response to cancer affords both the opportunity and challenge to make creative choices. Not 'Why me, O God?' but 'What do You desire to teach me through this experience?'

"I believe it is to live life to its fullest, with intensity and passion, to confront the issue of my own mortality by accepting God's will for my life prayerfully and with great joy. The joy comes through giving freely of one's self, dispersing fear, forgiving all, loving much, and 'letting go' of those material treasures that were previously impediments. The creative choice is: Love with all one's heart and soul, thank God all the day through and share his love with everyone.

"When I considered all the undeserved gifts (i.e., those things we couldn't possibly 'earn') that God has put into our lives — the undeserved blessings, undeserved persons, undeserved circumstances, I began to understand that my mission here is to express God's love and concern for other persons and in every circumstance of my life. That is how each of us can set this paradigm— this new, creative way of thinking — in motion.

"I am convinced that those of us with real meaning in our lives do better, have longer and fuller lives. I like Stephen Strum's description of 'holistic' medicine. He speaks of the 'holistic pie', with slices representing genetics, nutrition, conventional therapies, mind-body relationships, exercise, immunology, eastern medicine, and spirituality. The crust of the pie, holding everything together, is symbolic of the Will to Live. Without a will to live, there is no passion, no fire that keeps you burning bright! So Dr. Strum posits, 'Men need a reason to justify their lives — what better way to justify living than by helping others?' Sometimes we need to ask ourselves, 'Why did our Creator put us here? And what is a <u>successful</u> life?' Emerson said of success:

> 'To laugh much and often, to win the respect of intelligent people and the affection of little children; to earn the appreciation of honest critics and endure the betrayal of false friends; to

> appreciate beauty; to find the best in others; to leave the world a bit better, whether by a healthy child, a garden patch, or a redeemed social condition; to know even one life has breathed easier because you have lived. This is to have succeeded.'

"And so, as we survivors carry on our support group activities with the very best programs we can devise — as we visit one-on-one, with care and compassion, those prostate cancer survivors who are ill at home — as we engage in lengthy 'telephone visits' with those men and their families who have perplexing personal questions and wish to draw on our experiences — as we sit as 'advocates' on the scientific peer review panels convened by the National Cancer Institute and the Department of Defense — as we endeavor to educate and raise awareness about this insidious disease by our outreach to civic groups — may we see this as helping our fellow man and our own cause, for, as we must already know, we are all very much intertwined.

"In the giving of ourselves to our neighbors, we not only enrich our own lives, we have set in motion the paradigm of prostate cancer. As Dr. Strum wisely observes, 'We must remember that we are each here to learn; this life is our teaching lesson.' I would add that it is also *a personal teaching mission for us*. Yes, prostate cancer has changed my life and can change yours. This will be measured by our responses to the journey we are now taking. By God's grace, I would offer these closing thoughts:

Through me let there be kind words,
A warm smile, a caring heart.
Through me let there be willingness
To listen and a readiness
To understand.
Through Me let there be dependability,
Steadfastness, trust, and loyalty.
Through me let there be compassion,
Forgiveness, mercy, and love.
Through me let there be every
Quality I find, O Lord, in Thee.
—Anon.

In a card dated January 31, 1999, I found Robert's seventh psalm. It reflected a New Year's resolution that must have been most pleasing to his Lord.

Psalm 7. Only In You, Lord Jesus

My sincerest desire this year is
to come only to You,
to put aside and reject everything else,
to stand before You,
to praise You and to wait patiently.
To be cleansed and healed of
this malignant disease, if it be Your will.

To accept graciously that cancer is a divine appointment to receive Christ's miracle of His life into my heart.
To do so gratefully
with courage and prayerfulness -
whatever relief or pain may ensue.

Not to waste my time any more
with words and actions
that do not count before You
or that lack personal integrity.

To pray for and receive your fresh grace daily;
To order my life in a new way,
to consider what forms me,
and how others are formed through me
and then to cast away or embrace more.

Let it become acutely visible in my life
that You are the pearl, my all in all,
for which I will give up everything,
including my right to my own self.

That in You is my treasure
and my heart, for I do love You.
And allow me to express that love effectively

to Your honor and glory
through Obedience to Your will.
Empower me to faithfully keep
my promises to You and to my dear
Gerda, thus fulfilling my
Covenant
to be a godly man.

One thing I ask for is that I may seek
to dwell in the house of the Lord,
there to behold the face of
my Lord
and bow down in worship before Him.

There is not treasure here on this earth
that equals one day with You, Lord,
and here in Your presence,
I know perfect joy.
I lift up my voice to adore You.

Lord, I want to be Your servant
more than anything at all,
just to know that I've been
faithful to Your call,
just to love You.
Lord, I do love You.

Worthy are You, Lord,
O worthy are You, Lord.

AMEN.

A young Robert Alexander taking weapons training. Believed to be at Parris Island, SC, ca. 1950.

On leave, with younger sister Bonnie and Freckles, ca. 1950-51.

Robert receiving an award, believed to be upon his retirement from the Marine Corps Reserves, 1966.

Robert and Gerda, 1989.

Robert and Gerda, outside their "English cottage" in Warren, NJ, before relocating to Newville, PA.

Robert and Gerda, outside their home in Newville.

Robert, sporting his "professorial gray beard," during mission trip to Haiti, March 1999

Robert and Gerda, 1999.

Chapter 10: "Discouragement" (Psalm 8)

"Moses returned to the Lord and said, 'O Lord, why have you brought trouble upon this people? Is this why you sent me? Ever since I went to Pharaoh to speak in your name, he has brought trouble upon this people, and you have not rescued your people at all.'" Exodus 5:22,23 NIV

On February 2, 1999, just two days after writing his seventh psalm, Robert had another PSA test. It showed an alarming jump to 22.6, indicating that the triple blockade therapy initiated in December was so far ineffectual. But there seems to have been no diminution of his activity.

With Jim's encouragement, Robert had gotten involved in prison ministry. He began by corresponding with several prisoners whom Jim had suggested. On February 19, he sent me a tape featuring Dennis Jernigan, who had become one of his favorite Christian musicians. With it was a note, asking me to consider writing to one of the prisoners whom he'd befriended. To this, he added the following postscript:

> "In encouraging you to write, I only ask that if you feel the Lord's leading. In addition to Chris, I am also praying for and counseling another former prisoner, David, who is presently out on bail. Erik, I never in the world thought I'd be engaged in these endeavors – probably because I used to think I wouldn't have much to say or offer these men. But often they are much more broken and vulnerable

> than I believe I may have been. Anyway, the Spirit is doing the leading. What marvelous surprises the Lord has new for us every day."

In the face of his trials, Robert continued to draw strength and comfort from his faith, from Gerda and from his Thursday morning fellowship group. He had found a strong kindred spirit in the person of Jim Small, and they became accountability partners in the best sense of the word. Later that month, in his own inimitable fashion, Robert formalized their covenant relationship in another of his trademark cards. Side 1 of the card began:

A Covenant between

Robert Alexander & Jim Small

before their Sovereign Lord

Below this were verses from one of Robert's favorite hymns:

Jesus, I live to Thee,
The loveliest and best;
My life in Thee, Thy life in me,
In Thy blest love I rest.

Jesus, I die to Thee,
Whenever death shall come;
To die in Thee is life to me,

In my eternal home.

Whether to live or die,
I know not which is best;
To live in Thee is bliss to me,
To die is endless rest.

Living or dying, Lord,
I ask but to be Thine;
My life in Thee, Thy life in me,
Makes heaven forever mine.

"The Mercersburg Academy Hymn"
by Henry Harbaugh (1817-1867)

The text of the covenant appeared on Side 2:

"Courage, endurance, and
perseverance for daily exercise"

Covenant

Between Robert Alexander
and James Small
before Our Sovereign Lord

Witnesseth,

That Robert hereby promises to exercise every day when at home and also, insofar as possible, when away from home.

To keep in regular touch with Jim, as he directs, reporting on the progress of his exercise program. To accept and respect suggestions from Jim regarding this program. That Jim hereby promises to be an Encourager as well as Mentor to Robert by inquiring from time to time about the specifics of such exercise program, and to offer guidance and support. To also take note periodically of Robert's physical improvement and offer advice.

That both Robert and Jim hereby do covenant and promise to keep each other jointly in their daily prayers to the Lord, expectantly seeking His guidance to mutually edify and encourage each other, in season and out, as godly men who truly desire to be authentic Promise Keepers.

Signature of Robert: Robert Alexander

Signature of Jim: James Small

Date: February 20, A.D. 1999

As iron sharpens iron, so a man sharpens the countenance of his friend. Proverbs 27:17
A friend loves at all times and a brother is born for adversity. Proverbs 17:17

On the third and fourth sides of the cards, Robert included no fewer than twenty-two "suggestions for intercessory prayer." Among them:

> "Ask the Lord to lead you to place your trust in Him even as you dream tonight. Ask Him to give you the strength to trust your hidden thoughts to Him. Ask Him to give you perseverance for physical exercise.
>
> "Ask the Holy Spirit to visit you in your dreams and remind you of what your redemption really means. Ask Him to help you see yourself fit!
>
> "Ask the King to show you your place in His kingdom—as one of His children—even as you sleep. Ask Him for strength to do the exercises.
>
> "As you go to rest, allow the Holy Spirit to sing over the fears, anxieties, or concerns of your life. Ask Him to wash your heart with the melodies of grace so that your soul and body will awake refreshed and looking forward to experiencing more of His grace!
>
> "Ask the Lord to help you rest in His artistic hand tonight. Allow Him to show you some new aspect of His creative process in your life that you have not seen before. Ask Him to specifically show you a 'new you.'
>
> "Ask the Lord to remind you of some of the ways He has loved you even when you did not love Him. Ask Him to reassure you exercise is good!

> "Ask the Lord to heighten your level of understanding of how much you were forgiven. Then ask him to help you learn to express your love for Him accordingly. Ask Him to show you how He wants you to improve your body.
>
> "Ask the Lord to give you a renewed vision of how He might declare His glory and majesty through your life, so that when you awaken there will be no doubt about who He is and whose you are! 'I'll have a new body, a new life!'

He ended with, "Hallelujah! Praise the Lord!"

Despite his worsening condition, Robert volunteered for a mission trip to Haiti in March of 1999. Upon his return, he enthusiastically shared his feelings about it in a group e-mail message. However, he also showed some concern about his most recent PSA test, taken shortly before his departure. The reading had jumped again, to 29.1.

> "Many of you followed us with your prayers for our 15-member Haiti Mission Team from Falling Spring Church, March 2-10, 1999. It was with joy that I could say the final results of this mission filled the members of our team with gladness in challenges met, good fellowship, self-assessment, and much spiritual refreshment. We each experienced 'Joy in the Journey,' as we worked hand in hand with our Haitian brothers and sisters. In

short, we had a 'Message' and we endeavored to live that 'Message' each and every day.

"Back here on the 'home front,' today's visit to the urologist brought news that my PSA has again run up 7 points, this time to 29.1. Therefore, another bone scan and CT scan have been ordered, to be done next Tuesday, March 23. Also, a consultation with a leading oncologist in Harrisburg has been scheduled for Monday, March 29 to review second-line courses of treatment, including possible gene vaccine and/or anti-angiogenesis therapy (possibly in some trials at Johns Hopkins).

"It would be appreciated if you might remember this humble servant in your prayers, specifically that the cause(s) of rise in the prostate specific antigen may be pinpointed and that a promising new second-line defense course of action may be found. If you would be inclined to send any message 'us-ward,' that'd be a great encouragement, too!

"In closing may I encourage you to pick up your Bible and read Ephesians 3:14-21, which I think would be a beautiful colophon to this E-mail message.

"Blessings and thank you. By God's grace, ROBERT"

Robert underwent the bone and CT scans at Holy Spirit Hospital in Camp Hill on the 23rd as scheduled. Five days later, on Palm Sunday, he was both upbeat and reflective as he wrote:

> "This is the special day on which we were presented as new members at the Falling Spring Church, a day on which to wave palms in joyful processional, to sing praises with grateful hearts as the youth choir joined voices with the senior choir in Faure's 'The Palms.' It was a day also to celebrate at a splendid luncheon reception and be welcomed with warm wishes and smiles – a day when sunlight broke through the cloud cover with almost perfect timing as church let out!
>
> "These thoughts, which began running through my mind after we had sung the choral benediction ('The Lord bless you and keep you') I feel privileged to share with you:
>
> "I can't number the times I have wished God would hurry up – with an answer to my prayers – with a bailout in the midst of my muddle – with a fresh sense of His working in my life. But if there is one well-established principle in Scriptures, it is dramatically demonstrated in Jesus' experience: You can't rush a resurrection!
>
> "If I am walking in the simple path of God's will for me, 'I can never be conquered by anything. I may be down, but I'm not out!' He will get me up again, and He says when it will be – on the count of three!

"Consider with me: If Jesus could have called for angels to spare Him the suffering of the Cross, don't you think He could have called for an early deliverance from death? The message of His submission to the Father's timing as well as the Father's plan is profound in its application to my life (and yours).

"I've learned not to attempt a humanly energized 'bounce-back' from those circumstantial 'knock-downs' I've encountered. God has His own kind of 'mandatory nine-count'; it's a third-day rising for everyone who will wait for His moment of miracle deliverance!

"In entrusting everything concerning my case to Jesus, then the entire matter is sealed and delivered in advance – in His resurrection. The message is this: As surely as Jesus rose on time, our triumph will be on schedule also. Lazarus' schedule probably seemed a day or two late to him, too.

"As we move into Holy Week, isn't it great to know we really have the life of God in us, the power that made all the universe with just a word, and that He came to live in us abundantly? Shouldn't we shake off all the impedimenta (cares, worries, concerns) which prevent us from fully experiencing this transforming joy in our everyday lives!

"Tomorrow is the long awaited consultation with a leading medical oncologist in Harrisburg. We go there trusting with confidence that everything is indeed in the Lord's hands and under His timing. Thus far, there seem to be glimmers of good news.

"More thoughts later.... may God's richest blessings be with you and yours this day and every day of this week. May it be so in your life and in ours! By God's grace, ROBERT (and Gerda) Col. 3:17."

About this time, Robert also sent the following Easter greeting to Chris and Jeffery, two of the prisoners he had been praying for and corresponding with:

"Can anything separate us from the love Christ has for us? That's what we want to know! Does God really love us forever? Not just on Easter Sunday when our shoes are shined and our hair is combed.

"We want to know (deep within, don't we really want to know?) how does God feel about me when I'm a jerk! When I snap at anything that moves; when my thoughts are gutter-level; when my tongue is sharp enough to slice a rock. How does He feel about me then?

"That's the question. Can I drift too far? Wait too long? Slip too much? Did I out-sin the love of God? Well, the answer is found in one of life's sweetest words — GRACE! (Rom. 8:35,38,39). You can't fall beyond His love! Praise God that He who first made you and me is strong enough to sustain you and me. (Rom. 5:1,2.) Always and forever!

"With love, from your brother in Christ, *Robert*"

The long-awaited consultation with the oncologist, Dr. Robert A. Gordon, proceeded as scheduled, on Monday, March 29. Robert's medical log stated: "Results of Scans basically clear: CT scan showed single gallstone; Bone Scan report indicated 'tiny focus of possible metastatic activity on left acetabulum.' Dr. Gordon requested an additional x-ray of the pelvic area."

Robert's growing concern about his medical condition was revealed in an e-mail message just four days later, when he was responding to a prayer partner's inquiry about his specific requests:

> "You said in a recent message to be specific about prayers. Here are three requests:
>
> 1. "Please pray specifically that my letters to two prisoners (Chris at Rockview State Penitentiary and David at Cumberland County Prison) and the counseling of Jim Small, my brother in Christ out here, may be an encouragement and a blessing to them, as well as to all those convicts to whom Chris and David will be witnessing.
>
> 2. "Please also pray that our little Blue Mountain Fellowship on Thursday mornings may grow beyond our initial 4-6 guys – that we may be empowered

and set on fire to reach other men for Jesus Christ!

3. "Finally, for myself, please pray for healing and wholeness for me, specifically that the tiny 'probable bone metastasis' (that's what they term it) may be touched and healed by the power of the Holy Spirit! I can say this because I believe Christ's death on the wondrous cross is the basis for divine healing and I choose His supernatural power to supplement my doctor's treatments.

"I recall the watchword of our Haiti Mission Team in early March – 'The Joy is in the Journey.' And so it is for all of you and us who are washed in the blood of Christ and have experienced the marvel of new birth in Him. We pray for fresh grace daily not only for ourselves but for you, also. Blessings this day, tomorrow especially, and every day. Alleluia! Amen!

"By God's grace, ROBERT! (Phil. 3:7-11)"

The next entry in Robert's medical journal reflected another change in his therapy, as well as his increasing concern:

"As of April 5, 1999, discontinued taking the anti-androgen Eulexin, but continued with the

> Lupron and Proscar. Called Prostate Cancer Research Institute, Marina del Rey, CA for copies of PCR Insights, edited by Stephen B. Strum, M.D.[13] Spoke with Harry Pinchot, Dr. Strum's medical research assistant, who became the second person to urge me to see Dr. Snuffy Myers about second-line defense modalities. The first was Earl E. Twiss, Jr., of Chambersburg, PA, one of Snuffy's patients and a facilitator of our US TOO! Group at Chambersburg Hospital."

The same day, he sent a follow-up fax to Harry Pinchot. While concerned about his own condition, he didn't miss a chance to put in a plug for his Coalition, while seeking Dr. Strum's support!

> "Hello Harry!
>
> "Thank you for calling me back today and giving me your candid views about Casodex and Eulexin in cases where one has possibly/probably become hormonally refractory. I appreciate the fact that Snuffy Myers is right on the cutting edge and will endeavor tomorrow morning to reach his office. I need to arrange something as soon as possible, for on Thursday and Friday I'll be down in Bethesda serving on an NCI special emphasis panel.
>
> "When I talked with Jim Williams tonight and conveyed your greetings, he was delighted

to know we had talked. Jim said you really knew whereof you spoke, based on your personal experience. I didn't get the new address of your office, which I'll need to send off the priority mail packet tomorrow. Could you fax me that address and also your Email address?

"Herewith I am faxing some material on 'A Pilot Plan for Pennsylvania' which our Pennsylvania Prostate Cancer Coalition (a voluntary association, acting as an umbrella group for US TOO! And M2M support groups) wants to develop and set in motion. We're in the process of seeking funding to underwrite some segments of the program. I am indebted to Dr. Strum for having written 'The Paradigm of Prostate Cancer,' which was the genesis for our own efforts here in the Keystone State!

"Very best wishes.....and 'Keep Smilin'!'

Sincerely,
Robert"

The next day, Robert made a call to Dr. Myers office and got an appointment for April 25, in Charlottesville, Virginia. Apparently, during his conversation with Harry Pinchot, Robert had learned that one of the "second-line defense modalities" Harry had referred to was PC-SPES,[14] which Harry was taking himself.

Despite his worsening condition, Robert participated in an NCI panel in Rockville, Maryland on April 8th and 9th, then proceeded directly to Arlington, Virginia, for an NPCC meeting on the 12th. Given this second golden opportunity, Gerda and Jim Small finished their garage cleaning and filled the truck a second time!

Shortly after his return from these engagements, Robert made the following entry in his medical log: "Began PC-SPES @ dosage 6 capsules daily." His communications with Harry Pinchot had helped convince him to obtain this prescription from Dr. Owens.

On April 19, Robert sent a note of encouragement to one of my close friends in Annapolis, Steve Uhthoff, who was undergoing diagnosis following a test showing an elevated PSA:

> "Dear Steve: Thanks so much for your message. Yeah, a biopsy isn't all that much fun, I know! It'll be somewhat uncomfortable, but the results will be most important for you to know, especially the Gleason score![15] Be assured that I am praying for you and I have asked several brothers in Christ in our Blue Mountain Fellowship to also keep you in their prayers. I pray 2 Peter 1:2 for you, that your knowledge of God and of Jesus our Lord will flood all over you with grace and peace. If you will E-mail me your mailing address, I'll be glad to send along some material I've gotten together in my support group work, which may be helpful in the days ahead. I just learned today that my PSA has risen to 35.9, another seven-point rise since last month. We're a bit anxious but trusting always in our Lord's

promises that He will provide! Much love in Christ from your brother-in-Christ, ROBERT"

Robert's medical log began to have a quick succession of entries and seems to reflect some spirited dialogue with his HMO:

> "On April 26, 1999 had second consultation with Dr. Robert A. Gordon, medical oncologist at Pinnacle Polyclinic Hospital, Harrisburg, PA. He again suggested I consider being entered in a randomized, double-blinded clinical trial involving chemotherapy (mitoxantrone and prednisone) and AG3340, a novel inhibitor of selected matrix metalloproteinases with anti-angiogenesis properties. I respectfully declined this trial at this time, indicating I wanted to experiment for several months with PC-SPES. He wishes to see me in 6 weeks and have another Bone Scan done in 3 months.
>
> "On April 28, 1999 Nina Fehnel, an oncology nurse at Aetna US HealthCare called, re. letter we had asked Dr. Binder to apply for their National Medical Excellence Program to go out of network for consultation with Dr. Snuffy Myers at U.Va.......She phoned about the rationale for consulting Dr. Myers, indicating that Dr. Myers' AA did not seem familiar with my request for a consultation. Further noted that while Aetna may okay the U.Va.

> consultation, alternatively, they may wish me to accept a substitute second opinion consultation with Dr. Mario Eisenberger at Johns Hopkins or Dr. Steven Hahn at the Hospital of the University of Pennsylvania, both of whom are within their network."

At this point, nearly three years after his initial diagnosis, Robert had become an authority on prostate cancer. While he continued to counsel and encourage others, he began to realize that he might be losing his earthly battle. Gerda recalls that his rapidly increasing PSA readings were a primary cause for concern. It was on a page dated April 26-29, 1999, that I found the first writing of Robert's Eighth Psalm, which he'd simply entitled, "Discouragement." He began by reflecting on the following passage about Moses and applying it to his own personal situation:

> *"Moses returned to the Lord and said, 'O Lord, why have you brought trouble upon this people? Is this why you sent me? Ever since I went to Pharaoh to speak in your name, he has brought trouble upon this people, and you have not rescued your people at all.'"* Exodus 5:22,23 (NIV)

Psalm 8. Discouragement

Here in this passage I find a discouraged Moses, complaining to God.

It shows me it's important that we approach
God with integrity
in an attitude of humility.
Because we fear making a negative
confession, we sometimes cross the line of
honesty into the line of denial and delusion.

Let me be honest. God already knows what I
am feeling about cancer and the family
stress it kindles
when my PSA keeps going up and down,
when my support group seems to have let me
down.
God can handle our anger, complaints, and
disappointments.
He really understands us.
He is aware of our human frailties
(Ps. 103:14)
and can be touched with the feelings of our
infirmities (Heb. 4:15).
Sometimes in the midst of discouragement
and dejection, it is difficult to remember that
I have ever known any Scripture.
I therefore purpose to read aloud this prayer
daily until I really recognize afresh the
reality of God's Word
in my very spirit, soul, and body.

I must remember that God is watching
over His Word to perform it. (Jer. 1:12).
And I truly believe He will perfect
all that which concerns me. (Ps. 138:8).

My Prayer:

Lord, sometimes I don't understand why You
have allowed this malignancy to assail me.
It seems that after I really accepted Jesus
into my heart,
and began to follow You in obedience,
that this disease was manifested in my life.
The more I've struggled, the more I've felt I
may be exhausting the possibilities for
changing this situation through Your
healing.
And yet, I believe!
Help me overcome my unbelief!
All things are not possible with man,
but I believe all things are possible with You.
I therefore humble myself,
bowing on my knees before You,
and I pray You will lift me up.

I have a great High Priest Who has gone
through the heavens,

Jesus Your Son, and I hold firmly to the faith I profess.
My High Priest is able to sympathize with my weaknesses.
He was tempted in every way, just as I am—- yet He was without sin.
I approach Your throne of grace with confidence, so that I may receive mercy and find grace with confidence, to help me in this time of need.

In the face of discouragement, disappointment, and anger, I choose to believe that Your Word to Moses is Your Word to me.
You are mighty to deliver.
Because of Your mighty hand, You will drive out the forces that have set themselves up against me.
You are the Lord, Yahweh, the Promise-Keeper, the Almighty One.
You appeared to Abraham, to Isaac, and to Jacob,
and established your Covenant with them.
Father, I believe that You have heard my cries and my groaning.

I will live to see Your promises of deliverance
and healing fulfilled in my life.
You have not forgotten one word of Your promise;
You are a Covenant-Keeper!
You have redeemed me with an outstretched arm and
with mighty acts of judgment.
You have taken me as Your own, and You are my God.
You are a Father to me.
You have delivered me from the past that held me in bondage
and translated me into the Kingdom of love, peace, joy, and righteousness.

Father, what You have promised, I will go
and possess, in the name of Jesus.
I am willing to take the chance,
to take the risk,
to get back into the good fight of faith.
It is with patient endurance and steady,
active persistence that I must run the race,
the appointed course that is set before me.
I rebuke the spirit of fear, for I am established in righteousness.

I am more than conqueror through Him Who loves me and redeemed me.
In Christ's name I pray. Alleluia.
Amen. Amen. Amen.

Love, Robert,
Your new Creation.

References: Mark 9:24; Luke 18:27; I Pet. 5:6; Heb. 4:14-16; Ex. 6:3,4; Gen. 49:22-26; I Kings 8:56; Deut. 26:8; Col. 1:13; Rom. 5:20; I Tim. 6:12; Heb. 12:1; Isaiah 54:14-16; Rom. 8:37

Chapter 11: "Are You Still With Me, Jesus?" (Psalm 9)

> *"...Be content with what you have, because God has said, 'Never will I leave you; never will I forsake you.'"* Hebrews 13:5 (NIV)

Despite his medical setbacks, Robert continued to encourage others. On May 1, 1999, he sent this message to his sister-in-law:

> "Dear Barbara,
>
> "Today I seem to be tolerating the new chemotherapeutics much better. Still impotent physically in a certain sense — as Jim says, 'You'll get over that!' — but 'empowered' and fit nonetheless for the Lord's service.
>
> "I pray for you always, for your recovery and healing. I pray also for our families and our churches and all the unexpected saints and sinners our gracious Lord puts into our daily lives! For the spontaneous expressions of His love and for our willingness to respond openly and without reservations.
>
> "In all this Gerda joins me in these thoughts and prayers.
>
> "By God's grace, Robert
>
> May 1, 1999"

On May 5, he sent the following message in one of his cards to Chris Hess, the inmate at Rockview State Prison he had asked me to write several months earlier:

> "To Chris, my dear Brother in Christ,
>
> "What a precious gift and blessing it was to receive your beautiful letter today! When I read it the first time, I wept! And the second time also! And when Gerda read it, there were tears of joy! I thank you for your effectual prayers in the name of our Lord Jesus Christ. Chris, I did fall on my face before God and thanked Him for your precious love and for our redemption and healing and release through the blood of our Lord Jesus. That very moment there was a surge of peacefulness I could feel washing over me from head to toe. I thank the Holy Spirit for giving you His word **to** me and **for** me. I remember the lady Sara, about whom you wrote earlier and I pray the Lord will continue moving in her life. I haven't yet contacted her, but I will try to do so soon. I can't begin to express my appreciation for your words of comfort and healing. You are a very dear brother indeed and I love you, Chris. In the car I put on a worship and praise tape and sang praises to our King. It was wonderful! Chris, forgive my rambling thoughts — I couldn't wait to write and thank you. I praise God for you as that special person he has placed in my life for prayer, nurture and love.

> Thank you, dearest Jesus, My Lord, My God, My All. In Christ's love, your brother, Robert"

The card also contained the following message, along with Robert's ninth psalm:

> "I wrote this some months ago when I felt assailed by the evil one and had moments of anguish and even honest doubts."

Psalm 9. Are You Still With Me, Jesus?

Are you still with me, dear Jesus?
Perhaps I am to learn
that if I share my thoughts with another person,
this sharing may already change those thoughts?

Perhaps the moment has come
for me to enter my thoughts much more deeply than before,
to penetrate them
and to find their hidden motives.
I notice
that I want to share with others
much too quickly,
and that my feelings and thoughts
perhaps remain superficial because of it,

because talking often simplifies things
beyond the point to which they should be
simplified?

Dear Jesus, You stand across from me:
You let me think my thoughts to the end.
You do not interrupt me.
You do not even stop
that which might go in the wrong direction.
You do not hold me back
from entering something more dangerous,
but rather You give me the freedom
in which I may become truly independent.
And yet, You make it clear to me
that there are no half-measures,
that ultimately I must be totally immersed
into your dying
if I want to live in You.
I love You, Lord Jesus Christ! I claim Your
healing.
Alleluia. Amen.
—Your new creation called Robert

Chapter 12: "My Faith in You" (Psalm 10)

> *"Does the clay say to the Potter, 'What are you making?' Does your work say, 'He has no hands?'"*
> Isaiah 45:9b (NIV)

In the face of his discouragement, Robert continued to pray. One of his prayers was committed to writing in a message sent on May 17, 1999:

> "Father, I thank You that I have been delivered from the power of darkness and translated into the Kingdom of Your dear Son. I commit to live free from worry in the name of Jesus, for the law of the Spirit of life in Christ Jesus has made me free from the law of sin and death. Father, I delight myself in You, and You perfect that which concerns me. I thank You for these brothers in Christ who have been praying on my behalf and I ask that You grant them Your peace which passes all understanding in Jesus' name. Alleluia. Amen. By God's grace, ROBERT (Colossians 1:9-14)."

Then, just two days later, a joyful Robert sent this brief message to a long list of e-mail prayer partners:

> "After five weeks on PC SPES, this prostate cancer survivor is happy to report that his latest PSA, reported this afternoon, showed a decline

to 18.5 from April's high of 36! Hallelujah! Amen. By God's grace, ROBERT"

Seemingly renewed, on June 1st he shared his reflection on Pentecost with Mark Papera, Steve Uhthoff and me:

"Dear Brothers in Christ,

"As we begin the month of June, I would share with you these thoughts and bundle them together as a prayer offering for each of us in this season of Pentecost.

"I believe in the Holy Spirit, revealed in Scripture as personal and knowable; one in being with the Father and the Son, and even with them almighty, all-knowing, and ever-present. Because I believe this, I will worship and welcome Him in all aspects and affairs of my life.

"I believe in the Holy Spirit of love, who baptizes believers into the Body of Christ and through whose presence God's love is poured forth into our hearts. Because I believe this, I entertain the Holy Spirit's presence in my heart.

"I believe in the Holy Spirit of power, by whom the Father anointed Jesus' ministry, and with whom Jesus Himself baptizes all who will receive his impartation of ability. Because I believe this, I openly acknowledge my desire and express my request that Christ my Lord overflow my life with the promised Spirit from on high.

"Only prayer can bring about kingdom power. The love and power of the Father's will and rule can only be known here on earth if the redeemed of the Lord will call out for it. Prayer is no gamble. Prayer works (oh, yes, we praise the name of the Lord for evidences of it in our very lives)! 'Ask and you will receive' (Luke 11:9 paraphrase). Let us kneel before the Lord our Maker, giving thanks and praise and exalting Him for our redemption through the blood of our Lord Jesus Christ. Oh, taste and see that the Lord is good!

"I pray always for you and ask your earnest prayers for continued healing and wholeness.
Your brother in Christ, ROBERT (Psalm 148)."

A day later, he wrote to an eclectic group of prayer partners:

"June 2, 1999
"Dear Jim, Brad, Erik, Steve, Chris and David—all brothers in Christ!

"Greetings in the name of our Lord and Savior Jesus Christ! I wanted to share with each of you several thoughts I've had in recent weeks but have kept kind of bottled up. Have you ever done that? As we move into summer, I wanted to drop each of you a note.

"(1) MARK'S E-MAIL: Enclosed is an e-mail received from our prayer partner and brother in Christ, Mark Papera, who lives in New Jersey. I have been blessed before by the messages we've exchanged. Speaking of Pentecost, I was touched by these words Mark ties in with John Denler's Bible study on the Holy Spirit.

"(2) HAUNTED BY ANXIETY OR BY GOD? For June 2, Ozzie's[16] meditation cites Psalm 25:12, 'What man is he that feareth the Lord?' He points out that, 'If we are haunted by God, nothing else can get in, no cares, no tribulation, no anxieties. We see now why Our Lord so emphasized the sin of worry. How can we dare to be so utterly unbelieving when God is round about us? To be haunted by God is to have an effective barricade against all the onslaughts of the enemy.' He continues, 'In tribulation, misunderstandings, slander, in the midst of all these things, if our life is hid with Christ in God, He will keep us at ease. We rob ourselves of the marvelous revelation of this abiding companionship of God. [When] "God is our refuge" nothing can come through that shelter.'

"(3) HEALING MINISTRIES. In his excellent book, *Christian Healing,* Mark A. Pearson says that all those involved in the healing ministry should have a 'spiritual director.' Might this

> not apply to other Christians as well? Spiritual direction is not teaching, counseling, or training for ministry. It is, for example: *Helping one discern the movement of the Holy Spirit in his/her life. Giving assistance to help one reflect and grow in his/her walk with God. Helping one examine his/her prayer life to see how it might be improved. Being present to another in time of vulnerability. Becoming a spiritual friend and prayer partner.* This kind of 'direction' it would seem to me could be important because it helps us become whole in body, mind and spirit, and it assists us in resisting the forces of evil which are ever present, none more so than when we are in ministry to one another. Anybody have thoughts for me in this area?
>
> "I pray God's richest blessing for you this day and every day. II Corinthians 2:14
>
> Your brother in Christ, Robert"

On June 5, Robert shared the following reflective meditation with a larger group of his e-mail prayer partners:

> "LOOK AT US!" — *"And fixing his eyes on him, with John, Peter said, 'Look at us.'"* (Acts 3:4).
>
> "In my readings recently I came across some comments by Lloyd Ogilvie which set me to thinking about our times and travails. Writing

nearly twenty years ago, Dr. Ogilvie pictured our world as 'a crippled world,' as he related the story of the lame man at the Temple, described in Acts 3:1-10. Isn't that picture even more true in these days? Daily this crippled world cries out, as surely as that lame man at the Gate called Beautiful. We are crippled not only in body, but also in spirit. I believe in our day we still come to the Temple steps:

> unable to love,
> unable to forgive,
> unable to relate deeply,
> unable to face our insecurities,
> unable to live out our deepest convictions in life,
> unable even to bring peace to our own little corner of this strife-filled world.

"The sickness of our world is only a reflection of our inner condition. It's the big picture of what is inside us all. The residue of the sickness of the ages is in all of us. We all need repentance, healing and release far more than the beggar on the steps needed to walk. (And it's available to each of us this day and every day as a free gift.)

"What can we say to a sick and troubled world? Can we say, 'Look at us? Look at the quality of new life in our faith we have discovered?' Can we say that we have the answer? Peter and John unashamedly asked the lame beggar to look at them. They did have an answer. That lame man fixed his gaze on the two disciples, expecting to receive 'something' from them. Here is the story of a man wanting 'something' when what he needed was 'someone.' He must have been the first century spokesman of materialism for all ages. He expected something.

"The disciples had nothing to offer, but they had Someone. Yes, they had a Someone who had changed their lives and had given them purpose and power, healing and holiness, wisdom and will. They had no answer; they had THE answer. The world still yearns for something; we, who know, offer Someone—Christ Himself! Consider this motto: 'Live expectantly – walk purely – and serve faithfully.'
By God's grace, ROBERT."

On June 12, Robert sent a short reflection on Psalm 19:1-2: *"The heavens declare the glory of God; the skies proclaim the work of His hands. Day after day they pour forth speech; night after night they display knowledge."* It brought immediate recollections of "The Heavens Are Telling the Glories of God" from Haydn's *Creation*, which we had sung together in our church choir in New Jersey. He wrote:

> "THOUGHTS ABOUT TODAY'S VERSE…God's voice is always speaking. His witnesses give testimony to His glory, majesty and creative grace. The universe shouts with joy because behind its intricate beauty and power is the One who gave it life, purpose, and intention.
>
> "MY PRAYER…O Great God and Creator of the countless heavens and our own small, blue planet, thank you for noticing the heart cries of one so small in a universe so large. I love You, admire You, trust You, and worship You with wonder. Be exalted in my life, by words, and my deeds this day. In Jesus name I pray. Amen."

Two weeks later, on June 26, he shared another brief meditation from the "Desert Psalm," which had also been the subject of one of our choral pieces:

> "Psalm 63:1-2 says, *'O God, You are my God; Earnestly will I seek you; My soul thirsts for You; My flesh longs for You in a dry and thirsty land where there is no water. So I have looked for You in the sanctuary, to see Your power and Your glory.'*
>
> "I will offer praise to the Lord, asking for greater faithfulness in sharing Christ, for the Lord's work in our families, for our friends and neighbors, and for those in bondage and in prisons.

'Lord, I desire to live as one
Who bears a blood-bought name,
As one who fears but grieving Thee,
And knows no other shame.'

"Father of light, of love and mercy, please remove from my heart any cynicism or delight in seeing any others around me fall. Instead, let me be a rescuer rather than a neglecter. I ask your grace to be seen in my friendships. Through Jesus I pray.
—-Robert, your new creation."

Less than two weeks later, on June 29, an upbeat Robert updated us again on his medical condition:

"Hello everybody! Just wanted to let you know there's a new PSA reading as of yesterday. It's now down to 11.0, which represents about a 59% drop from last month. In May, it was 18.5, about a 51% decline from the April reading of practically 36. Mid-April was when I began my experiment with PC SPES (under doctors' guidance) at a recommended median dosage. Gerda and I are thankful for this gift of answered prayer. We want to thank you, too, for thinking of us and praying for us. (Psalm 138:8.)"

His encouraging medical news seemed to put Robert on another upswing! The messages of encouragement and inspiration to his prayer partners continued. On July 7, he wrote:

> "My dear Christian brothers,
> "He's always there.
> That's what makes any season of trial,
> any call to faith,
> any burden of responsibility a glory-time.
> Jesus is there.
> Not a doctrine about Him.
> Not an idea of what He's like.
> Not a memory of some past experience.
> No. Just Him.
> Jesus, my living Lord – here in the present tense!
> Alleluia!
> By God's grace, ROBERT"

Two days later, he encouraged us to reflect on a passage from Paul's letter to the Ephesians:

> *"Now to Him who is able to do immeasurably more than all we ask or imagine, according to His power that is at work within us, to Him be glory in the church and in Christ Jesus throughout all generations, for ever and ever! Amen."* Ephesians 3:20-21 (NIV)

> "THOUGHTS ABOUT THIS VERSE...Of all the names for God in the Bible, this is my favorite: 'Him who is able to do immeasurably more...' Our God is the same God who parted

the Red Sea and fed 5,000 or more on a green hillside with only a couple of sardine sandwiches. He longs to do much more than we ask and imagine, but most of us (including this humble servant) haven't really given Him much of a challenge. Dream big dreams for God. Then hang on!

"MY PRAYER...Almighty and awesome God, do in our day what You did in past days. Give us faith to believe and then amaze us at the smallness of our faith. Give us vision to see Your plan and do greater things. We ask this, not for ourselves or our experience, but for Your glory and the salvation of our world. In the strong name of our Lord Jesus Christ. Amen.
"By God's grace, ROBERT."

On the week-end of July 23-24, Robert returned to Veterans Stadium in Philadelphia for another Promise Keepers conference. This time he was accompanied by Jim Small. They had arranged in advance to sit with Mark Papera, by now a soul brother and intimate prayer partner, in spite of the fact that Robert was meeting him for the first time. Jim describes the week-end simply as an "affirmation" for Robert.

I found Robert's tenth psalm in a card he sent during this month of July 1999. It is unclear whether it was written before or after the Promise Keepers event. It reflects on texts from the books of Isaiah and Romans:

"Does the clay say to the Potter, 'What are you making?' Does your work say, 'He has no hands?'"-Isaiah 45:9b (NIV)

".....But who are you, O man, to talk back to God? Shall what is formed say to Him who formed it, 'Why did you make me like this?' Does not the potter have the right to make out of the same lump of clay some pottery for noble purposes and some for common use?" — Romans 9:20-21 (NIV)

Psalm 10. My Faith in You

My faith in You, dear Jesus,
is like clay on the wheel of the potter;
formed and fired.

In constant change it is molded
to create me in Your image,
a likeness of praise.

My will is fixed on You
and when it wavers
I lose the ground under my feet.

I am joined to You by my sin
and by your death,

bound together in the tumble through life.

Lord, I am anchored in You
like a tree in the earth,
held between life and death,
in the ground of faith
which You are.

Chapter 13: "Father, By Your Grace..." (Psalm 11)

"Therefore, my brothers, be all the more eager to make your calling and election sure. For if you do these things, you will never fall, and you will receive a rich welcome into the eternal kingdom of our Lord and Savior Jesus Christ." – 2 Peter 1:10-11 (NIV)

Robert continued to send e-mails and cards of encouragement to men afflicted with prostate cancer. He also did this with his growing list of prayer partners. On July 28, 1999, he sent the following brief e-mail message:

> "As we thrilled to Lance Armstrong's achievement in overcoming cancer and his come-back victory in the Tour de France, we remember how much of a journey we have yet to cover in finding a cure or cures for cancer. May we be inspired to press on and never give up hope!
> Godspeed, ROBERT"

Three days later, he again seized the opportunity for public advocacy as he followed up by writing to the editorial page director of *The Patriot-News* in Harrisburg:

> "As a four-year survivor of prostate cancer and an avid sports enthusiast, I watched with fascination and admiration as Lance Armstrong's ride to victory unfolded in France.

The hard work, the focus, the preparation and the teamwork required to win what is arguably the most difficult single athletic challenge in the world is a magnificent achievement on its own merits.

"But this is so much more to many people; Lance spoke so eloquently about the paralyzing fear each of us faces when confronted with a cancer diagnosis. The fact that his particular cancer was so far advanced, as his physician said, 'the worst,' shows us the bigger victory, the victory over fear, devastating illness, and the willingness of his former teammates to write him off.

"This achievement is a victory for all of us who fight this cancer battle every day, because it demonstrates what can be done! Let us not forget that Lance's victory over cancer was possible because of cancer research and highly skilled physicians. Nonetheless, we still lose nearly 560,000 Americans every year to some form of cancer – lives that could contribute so much to the common good.

"Cancer research is still woefully underfunded. The approximately $3 billion that the Federal government will invest in all forms of cancer research in 1999 only permits the National Cancer Institute to fund about 28% of the research grants approved in the peer review process; about 72% will go unfunded because of lack of resources.

> "Let's take the message of this wonderful victory to heart. Let's dedicate ourselves to making the defeat of cancer a national priority. Let's tell our legislators they can and should provide both the leadership and the funding to win this battle! It's a fight worth funding!
> Sincerely,
> ROBERT ALEXANDER
> Chairman of the Pennsylvania Prostate Cancer Coalition"

A week later, Robert passed on an inspiring story in this group e-mail message:

> "Hi All - This message encourages me as I endeavor to walk the talk! Amazing!
> READ THIS. LET IT REALLY SINK IN ...THEN CHOOSE HOW YOU START YOUR DAY TOMORROW...
>
> "Michael is the kind of guy you love to hate. He is always in a good mood and always has something positive to say. When someone would ask him how he was doing, he would reply, 'If I were any better, I would be twins!' He was a natural motivator. If an employee was having a bad day, Michael was there telling the employee how to look on the positive side of the situation. Seeing this style really made me curious, so one day I went up to Michael and asked him, 'I don't get it! You can't be a positive person all of the time. How

do you do it?' Michael replied, 'Each morning I wake up and say to myself, Mike you have two choices today. You can choose to be in a good mood or you can choose to be in a bad mood. I choose to be in a good mood. Each time something bad happens, I can choose to be a victim or I can choose to learn from it. I choose to learn from it. Every time someone comes to me complaining, I can choose to accept their complaining or I can point out the positive side of life. I choose the positive side of life.' 'Yeah, right, it's not that easy,' I protested. 'Yes, it is,' Michael said. 'Life is all about choices. When you cut away all the junk, every situation is a choice. You choose how you react to situations. You choose how people will affect your mood. You choose to be in a good mood or bad mood. The bottom line: It's your choice how you live life.'

"I reflected on what Michael said. Soon thereafter, I left the tower industry to start my own business. We lost touch, but I often thought about him when I made a choice about life instead of reacting to it. Several years later, I heard that Michael was involved in a serious accident, falling some 60 feet from a communications tower. After 18 hours of surgery and weeks of intensive care, Michael was released from the hospital with rods placed in his back. I saw Michael about six months after the accident. When I asked him how he was, he replied, 'If I were any better, I'd be twins. Wanna see my scars?' I declined to see his wounds, but did ask him what had gone through his mind as the accident took place. 'The first thing that went through my mind was the well-being of my soon to be born daughter,' Michael replied. 'Then, as I lay on the ground, I remembered that I had two choices: I could choose to live or I could choose to die. I chose to live.' 'Weren't you scared? Did you lose consciousness?' I asked. Michael continued, '... the paramedics were great. They kept telling me I was going to be fine. But when they wheeled me into the ER and I saw the expressions on the faces of the doctors and nurses, I got really scared. In their eyes, I read "he's a dead man." I knew I needed to take action.' 'What did you do?' I asked. 'Well, there was a big burly nurse shouting questions at me,' said Michael. 'She asked if I was allergic to anything. "Yes, I replied." The doctors and nurses stopped working as they waited for my reply. I took a deep breath and yelled, "Gravity." Over their laughter, I told them, 'I am choosing to live. Operate on me as if I am alive, not dead."

"Michael lived, not just due to the skill of his doctors, but also because of his amazing attitude. I learned from him that every day we have the choice to live fully. Attitude, after all, is everything.

"Godspeed, ROBERT"

Though it wasn't one of Robert's compositions, that story has had a continuing impact on me. Now, when I seem to find myself in a difficult situation, I remember that, as a Christian, I'm the child of a King…so if I were any better, I'd be twins!

On August 17, Robert shared how he had been impacted by his prayer group's recent study of the book of Colossians:

> "….Each of us was asked to give some personal testimony as to what this study had meant to us. Some guys had differing views about what was most important. For myself, I was led to say how perfectly tailored this book was to my spiritual needs right now.
>
> "In it, Paul refutes the Colossian heresy. In what I consider very beautiful language, Paul exalts Christ as the very image of God, the Creator, the preexistent sustainer of all things, the head of the church, the first to be resurrected, the fullness of the deity in bodily form, and the reconciler. Every time I read that first chapter, I get goose bumps! This part was the high point for me. When I re-read Col. 1:15-23, I wept as I remembered the impact those words have had in my life. For last July and again this July, as I knelt at Promise Keepers, I willingly rededicated my life to Jesus Christ – and both times my life has been changed, energized, and redirected!

"The warnings to guard against false teachers and the rules for holy living were likewise highly important. It's such a short book, but it's packed with 'nutrients' for our souls. Please do yourself a favor and read it. Tell me what you think. As oft I think of you, I pray for you from the heart! God's richest blessings – peace and joy!"

On August 20, he sent the following devotional reflection to his e-mail prayer partners:

> *"He who has the Son has life; he who does not have the Son of God does not have life."* —1 John 5:12
>
> "THOUGHTS ABOUT TODAY'S VERSE...This statement is both a reminder of God's glorious grace and also of our need to share that grace with others.
> "MY PRAYER...Father of all nations, resurrect in your people a desire to spread your grace to every language, tribe, nation, and people. Empower us with your Spirit so we will speak the Gospel of Jesus with boldness and respect to a world that does not know him. Use us to help others come to life in the Son! Through whom we pray. Amen.
> "Godspeed, ROBERT"

Three days later, on August 23, he reflected on a passage from Psalm 94:

"When I said, 'My foot is slipping,' your love, O Lord, supported me. When anxiety was great within me, your consolation brought joy to my soul." Psalm 94:18-19 (NIV)

"Upon reading this last night, I thought, While we are amazed at the vastness of God's reach and the awesome breadth of His power and the glorious sweep of His majesty, the incredible truth is His personal nearness to each of us. He chooses to know us and be actively involved in the trials and triumphs of each day with us. How will today, or tomorrow, be different because we are aware of His presence and companionship?

"This is my prayer today: O God who is near, please hear my heart. I am overwhelmed at Your presence near me and within me. The comfort You bring when I am under siege, the strength You offer when I am weak, the courage You give when I am under attack, and the hope You instill when all seems helpless – these gifts of Your presence are precious to me. Without Your presence I would not know where to go or why I am here. Thank you for knowing me. I look forward to knowing You one day just as You know me completely today. In the precious, strong name of Jesus Christ I pray. Alleluia. Amen. Amen.
Godspeed, ROBERT"

On September 4, Robert advised us of what appeared to be some encouraging medical news:

"Dear Mark, Ray, Steve, and Erik—

"When I went for my 3-month physical and Lupron injection on Friday, Dr. Owens asked me to guess my new PSA. In a few seconds, he broke the news: told me it was down to 9.0. 'Isn't that great!' he exclaimed. That's the backdrop for this brief message to Dietrich von Schwerdtner, who leads our Tuesday morning Bible study at Falling Spring. Since this tells the story, I wanted to share it with you and also let you know how much Gerda and I thank you for keeping us in your prayers.

"Dear von – Yes, isn't it wonderful to have a physician who is as enthusiastic and caring as Dr. Owens! Therefore, I will fall on my face before the Lord for his graciousness and favor! He has given me Jesus in whom I abide every day. He has tenderly guided and touched me during those times when no treatment seemed very responsive. And by the time I simply cried, 'Help, Lord,' (Psalm 12:1) He had already begun teaching me the lessons of love, patience, dependence, long-suffering, kindness and gentleness in my daily walk. Looking back over the crucial moments where things were held in the balance, I can see the Lord's fingerprints and His grace leading me to where I am today. So I would ask Him to make His

presence more powerfully known in my life as I seek His will and live to His glory. I thank you, also, for all your encouragement to me and our Tuesday morning Bible Study group!
By God's grace, ROBERT"

Robert seemed to have growing confidence in both the efficacy of PC-SPES, and in Dr. Myers, one of its most prominent proponents. On September 10, he sent me a short message to report that he and Gerda had been "out in Dayton, OH to actually see and hear Snuffy Myers (Dr. Charles E. Myers, Professor of Medicine and Director of Uva's Comprehensive Cancer Clinic) speak on Tuesday [September 7]. Meanwhile, at home the mailbox held a confirmation notice for the long-awaited 2nd opinion consultation with Snuffy on November 11!"

Heartened by his latest medical report, Robert continued his ministry activities. In early October, he and Jim Small attended a Prison Fellowship event at the State Correctional Institution in Dallas, Pennsylvania, where approximately forty percent of the inmates are lifers. Jim reports that this was another deeply moving experience, during which the Holy Spirit continued His work. Robert was also involved in the ambitious planning of a conference to be sponsored by his Pennsylvania Prostate Cancer Coalition in November. Still, he acknowledged the validity of an observation expressed by one of his new accountability partners – a prisoner! – as he wrote on October 17:

"Dear Brothers in Christ –

"I thank you for keeping me in your prayers and for your messages from time to time. These past few weeks have been exceedingly busy ones – three weeks ago, we participated on an ACS team in northwestern and north central PA, presenting the work done by PCa support groups; two weeks ago 17 of us were volunteers in the Prison Fellowship Ministry at SCI Dallas; a week ago Gerda and I celebrated our 30th anniversary at The Hershey Hotel, scene of our honeymoon in 1969; later in the week I was asked to attend an US TOO! regional directors conference in Chicago.

"Lest this sound like boasting, Jeffery took me down a peg or two. He's a believer at Dallas who has a strong faith and a perceptive eye. He wrote me a note cautioning me about such extensive busyness, praying that it wouldn't become an impediment in my walk with the Lord. Praise God for this fellow's insight and concern! Certainly God must want me to remember that, even though my cancer appears to be virtually in remission, he is giving me this added time to care for myself and my spouse as well as to minister to others."

Then, despite this admonition to himself, he continued with a meditation he'd prepared:

"*The Lord confides in those who fear him; he makes his covenant known to them. My eyes are ever on the Lord, for only he will release my feet from the snare."* — Psalm 25:14-15 (NIV)

"THOUGHTS ABOUT TODAY'S VERSE...Where does true deliverance come from? Only from our Sovereign King, the Lord of Hosts. Salvation is found in God through deep reverential respect for His holiness and might, through living in covenant relationship with Him, and through maintaining our focus on Him. Any other roads to salvation and deliverance are false and ultimately prove themselves to be a snare.

"MY PRAYER...Precious Father, you have done so much to save me. You who are so holy and righteous have reached down to take my hand. Teach me Your ways. Correct the wrongs in my life. Guide me into Your truth. I want to not only be saved from my sin, but from days of busyness, uselessness and frustration. Make me a vessel that can be used to honor You. I pray this prayer also for these brothers in Christ who are keeping Gerda and me in their prayers. I bless You for them and ask that they, too, may be vessels of honor and praise for You. Through Jesus, our precious Savior, I pray. Thank you, Father, thank you. Alleluia. Amen. Amen.
By God's grace, ROBERT"

On October 27, he sent the following message and rallying cry to a large group, including all of his prayer partners and everyone associated with his prostate cancer support groups:

> "Just when I was getting a bit discouraged about the slowness of our registrations for Nov. 20, along comes this powerful encouraging message from Ralph Valle in Phoenix! This first PPCC conference ought to be just the beginning! We ought to never give up hope that we're on the right track. When I re-read Ralph's message this morning it gave me a lump in my throat. He really hit the nail on the head. I'm grateful to him for reminding us that our four pillars are indeed worthy enough to be our guides all across the nation. Hey guys, let's get with it. As Ralph reminds us, 'Only God knows our time left on this earth. Apathy is rampant, but we cannot allow it to dissolve our resolve to persevere!'
> "Godspeed, ROBERT"

On the following day, in another large group e-mail message, Robert passed on some encouraging thoughts from a book he'd read:

> "For my dear brothers in Christ – May I offer you these words which have meant much to me, as a gift offering to you.
> Godspeed, ROBERT"

'CHANGE YOUR THOUGHTS AND YOU'LL CHANGE YOUR LIFE[17]

'Some people walk around all day like a powder keg ready to explode. If you find yourself letting anger rule your actions and ruin your day - or others around you - you need to re-evaluate your thinking. What you think determines how you feel, not the other way around.

- Nobody makes you mad. If someone is rude or demeaning, you do not have to respond in kind. Your actions and reactions are your choice. Nor are you at the mercy of all the pettiness, meanness, impatience, and anger of others. Besides, do you want to let someone else decide how you are going to act?

- You make you mad. The people and pressures in your life don't make you angry; something inside you makes you feel that way. When you change what you are thinking you can stop being angry.

- Reality is not what happens to you. Reality is what you think about what happens to you. You have little or no control over what happens to you, but God's grace gives you more control over what happens in you than you are willing to admit and accept. Epictetus, the first-century philosopher, said, when we meet with difficulties, become anxious and troubled, let us not blame others, but rather ourselves; that is, our ideas about things.

- Check what's in your mind. *"Son of man, have you seen what the elders of the house of Israel do in the dark, every man in the chambers of his imagery?"* (Ez. 8:12). What is going on in the chambers of your imagery?

- Wrong thinking is a sin problem. Acknowledge your misbeliefs, confessing them to God - and to someone who can pray for you. Repent, in the New Testament Greek, means literally to change your mind.

- Feed your brain. The Bible has the power to change your thoughts because it's God's Living Word, and it's the truth. It has the power literally to change your thoughts when you are powerless.

- Be a card-carrying Christian. Take a 3-by-5-inch card, and on one side write the scripture you find especially life-giving for your personal situation. On the other side write STOP! in large letters. Carry the card with you. When your thoughts start running away from you, pull out the card and read it to yourself - out loud if you can. Tell your brain: Stop thinking that way! Then turn the card over and review the Bible references. Read them again and again, many times a day if necessary. (Try Psalm 20:1-5.)

- Filter your thoughts through the Holy Spirit. I will ask the Father, Jesus promised, and He will give you another counselor to be with you forever - the Spirit of truth (John 14:16-17). You can tap into the power of God's wisdom and discernment if you will call upon the Holy Spirit to help you find the truth.

- Utilize crises. People change radically when the hurricanes of life blow through their brains. Hardship is the way the Lord disciplines us. *"My son, do not make light of the Lord's discipline, and do not lose heart when He rebukes you, because the Lord disciplines those He loves, and He punishes everyone He accepts as a son. Endure hardship as discipline."* Heb. 12:5-7 (NIV)'

"My prayer in closing: Eternal God, Almighty Father, Tender Shepherd, you already know

> my heart. You know where I struggle with sin, so please empower and forgive. You know my fears, so please encourage and strengthen me. You know my immaturity, so please nurture and cause me to grow. You know my weakness and my disease, so please comfort and heal me. But even if none of these are answered, I am still awed by the fact that You chose to know me. Thank you! In Jesus, name I pray. Amen.
> Your new creation, ROBERT"

On November 10, Robert received the results of another PSA test. It had risen to 10.1 from 9.1 two months earlier. This marked the first increase since he had begun using PC-SPES. However, he made no mention of this when, on November 13, he passed on a moving reflection on Veterans Day, again to a large group:

> "Even though this a day or two late, the thought is still vibrant and worth reading. We're proud to offer it to you.
> Godspeed, ROBERT"

> "Some veterans bear visible signs of their service: a missing limb, a jagged scar, a certain look in the eye.
> Others may carry the evidence inside them: a pin holding a bone together, a piece of shrapnel in the leg - or perhaps another sort of inner steel: the soul's ally forged in the refinery of adversity.

Except in parades, however, the men and women who have kept America safe wear no badge or emblem.

You can't tell a vet just by looking.

What is a vet?

He is the cop on the beat who spent six months in Saudi Arabia sweating two gallons a day making sure the armored personnel carriers didn't run out of fuel.

He is the barroom loudmouth, dumber than five wooden planks, whose overgrown frat-boy behavior is outweighed a hundred times in the cosmic scales by four hours of exquisite bravery near the 38th parallel.

She - or he - is the nurse who fought against futility and went to sleep sobbing every night for two solid years in Da Nang.

He is the POW who went away one person and came back another – or didn't come back AT ALL.

He is the Quantico drill instructor who has never seen combat – but has saved countless lives by turning slouchy, no-account rednecks and gang members into Marines, and teaching them to watch each other's backs.

He is the parade-riding Legionnaire who pins on his ribbons and medals with a prosthetic hand.

He is the career quartermaster who watches the ribbons and medals pass him by.

He is the three anonymous heroes in The Tomb Of The Unknowns, whose presence at the

Arlington National Cemetery must forever preserve the memory of all the anonymous heroes whose valor dies unrecognized with them on the battlefield or in the ocean's sunless deep.

He is the old guy bagging groceries at the supermarket - palsied now and aggravatingly slow - who helped liberate a Nazi death camp and who wishes all day long that his wife were still alive to hold him when the nightmares come.

He is an ordinary and yet an extraordinary human being - a person who offered some of his life's most vital years in the service of his country, and who sacrificed his ambitions so others would not have to sacrifice theirs.

He is a soldier and a savior and a sword against the darkness, and he is nothing more than the finest, greatest testimony on behalf of the finest, greatest nation ever known.

So remember, each time you see someone who has served our country, just lean over and say 'Thank You.' That's all most people need, and in most cases it will mean more than any medals they could have been awarded or were awarded.

Two little words that mean a lot, 'THANK YOU'.

Remember November 11th is Veterans Day"

On December 7, Robert and Gerda flew to Seattle for a twelve-day visit with Robert's sister Bonnie and her family.

During their stay, Robert managed to arrange a visit to a prominent clinical researcher, Dr. Gerald P. Murphy, who was engaged in a potentially breakthrough therapy for prostate cancer involving dendritic cells. Gerda recalls that Robert was heartened by this meeting and that they had arranged for a follow-up consultation. However, approximately a month later, Dr. Murphy fell ill and died during a trip to Japan.

Upon their return to Pennsylvania, Robert and Gerda learned the results of a PSA test he had taken shortly before their departure. It showed another increase, this time to 12.1. Less than three weeks later, on January 4, 2000, it had jumped alarmingly, to 19.1. Gerda recalls that about this time Robert went through a very difficult period, with a great deal of trouble sleeping. He wasn't sure how much of this may have been caused by side effects from his medication, but he apparently became quite distressed. There was increasing evidence that his most recent line of defense, PC-SPES, was no longer stemming the tide. In one of his cards written that month, he again included his psalm of discouragement, which he had written in April of the preceding year.

Yet on January 27, Robert sent another message of encouragement to Mark Papera, Steve Uhthoff and me, reflecting on Philippians 4:8:

> *"Whatever is true, whatever is noble, whatever is right, whatever is pure, whatever is lovely, whatever is admirable – if anything is excellent or praiseworthy – think about such things."*
> Philippians 4:8 (NIV)

"Phil Ware says that our actions follow our thoughts like a heat-seeking missile follows the exhaust of a jet fighter's engine. So, in a day when so much around us trains us to find the negative in life, we must aggressively think and pursue the character, the qualities, and the things of God's goodness.

"I would offer this prayer for myself and my brothers in Christ: Holy and Magnificent God, our Creator and Sovereign King, thank you for being better than anything this world can offer me. Thank you for giving me the promise of a better future than any human can imagine. Thank you for giving me a high calling. In Jesus' precious name I pray. Alleluia. Amen. Your new creation, ROBERT."

This was the last e-mail message I received from Robert for a period of more than five months. On February 6, he traveled by train from Harrisburg, via Philadelphia, to New York to participate as a cancer survivor advocate in an NCI Site Review Committee at Sloan Kettering. The conference was to last for three days. But on February 7, Robert was in obvious pain. Doctors in attendance noticed severe swelling in his legs, caused by lymphedema. They arranged for him to be driven to Penn Station for a return trip to Philadelphia. Gerda met him there, accompanied by a staff member from Green Ridge Village.

To address the lymphedema, Robert began another course of treatment at a hospital in Harrisburg. This involved special bandages and regular massages of his legs.

On February 11, he made what was to be the last entry in his medical log. It showed that his PSA had continued to increase, to 22.69.

Five days later, in the face of these latest reverses, Robert wrote what I believe was his last psalm. I found it in a card that cited an encouraging passage from 2 Peter 1:2-11. In this meditation, he seeks deliverance from "the sin of worry" so that he might "walk in that peace which passes all understanding in Jesus' name!" Despite his pain and anguish, Robert was now beginning to look forward to the "rich welcome into the eternal kingdom" promised by his Lord.

Like so many of Robert's other cards, this one began with the words from Daniel Gawthrop's "Sing Me to Heaven."

Psalm 11. Father, by Your Grace

Father, by Your grace, allow me
to live free from worry.

Heavenly Father, I thank You that I am being delivered from the power of darkness and translated into the Kingdom of Your dear Son. I commit to live free from worry in the name of Jesus, for the law of the Spirit of life in Christ Jesus has made me free from the law of sin and of death.

I humble myself under Your mighty hand
that in due time You may exalt me.
I cast the whole of my cares -
and I name them one by one -
all my anxieties, all my worries, all my
concerns, once and for all - on You.
You care for me affectionately and
care about me watchfully.
You sustain me.
You will never allow those who are
consistently righteous to be moved,
or to slip and fall!
Father, I delight myself in You, and believe
You will perfect that which concerns me!

I cast down imaginations and every high
thing that exalts itself against the knowledge
of You, and bring every thought to the
obedience of Jesus Christ,
my Lord and Savior.

I lay aside every weight and the sin of worry
which does so easily beset me -
by the blood of the Lord Jesus.

I run with patience the race that is set before me, looking unto Jesus, the author and finisher of my faith.

I thank You, Father, that You are able to keep that which I have committed unto You. I fix my mind on those things that are true, honest, just, pure, lovely, of good report, virtuous, and deserving of praise.

I let not my heart be troubled and I drive depression away. I want to abide in Your Words, and have Your Words abide in me. Therefore, Father, I do **not** *forget what manner of person I am.*

I look into the perfect law of liberty and continue therein, being **not** *a forgetful hearer, but a doer of the Word and thus blessed in my doing!*

Thank You, Father.
I want to be carefree.
So may I walk in that peace which passes all understanding in Jesus' name!

Alleluia. Alleluia.
Amen.
Amen.

Robert, Your new creation in
Jesus Christ.

Newville, PA – February 16, 2000

Chapter 14: "Barnabas"

"Joseph, a Levite from Cyprus, whom the apostles called Barnabas (which means Son of Encouragement), sold a field he owned and brought the money and put it at the apostles' feet." – Acts of the Apostles 4:36,37 (NIV)

I believe that every Christian man can benefit greatly from developing deep relationships with three types of other men: (1) a more mature Christian who can serve as a mentor, much as Paul was to Timothy; (2) a less mature Christian to mentor oneself, much as Timothy was to Paul; and (3) a peer who will both hold him accountable and offer encouragement in times of trial. I think the best New Testament model for this last individual is the man whom the apostles called Barnabas, the Son of Encouragement. A Barnabas is someone with whom you can share your innermost thoughts without fear of betrayal. He is someone who will hold you accountable in times of temptation and encourage you in times of trial. Most importantly, he is someone who will bare his own soul while he prays with you.

The preceding chapters bear ample testimony that, during the last years of his life, Robert Alexander *was* a Barnabas to at least three men – to Jim Small, to Mark Papera and to me. And I know that he was an encourager of many others. But now his final earthly chapter had begun.

On March 16, 2000, Robert was preparing for a Man to Man support group meeting he was to lead that evening. He dropped off some material with a local printer, then began to take a walk around the village with Gerda, an activity that had been encouraged by his physicians. Gerda recalls that he suddenly stopped and said, "I can't walk!" But after a short rest, he recovered sufficiently for them to get home. Robert then drove back to the printer to pick up his material. Upon returning home, he again experienced difficulty walking. He admitted to Gerda that he would be unable to attend and lead the group that night. It was the first Man to Man meeting he had missed.

In the face of these reversals, Robert continued to explore other avenues, including clinical trials for promising new drugs. On May 16, he initiated correspondence with Dr. Abdelaziz Elgamal at Northwest Biotherapeutics in Seattle. It demonstrated that he was still intellectually engaged in the search for a cure.

> "Dear Dr. Elgamal:
>
> "Thank you for your fax message containing the eligibility criteria. I am including with this message the following supplemental information:
> (1) Omega Medical Lab report dated March 11, 2000. If needed, we'll have another Health Screen report done. Please advise if I should do this.
> (2) Nuclide Total Bone Scan on March 23, 1999 at Holy Spirit Hospital, Camp Hill, PA. Is this recent enough for your consideration?

(3) CT Scan of Abdomen and Pelvis with Contrast Enhancement on March 23, 1999, at Holy Spirit Hospital, Camp Hill, PA.

Sincerely,
Robert"

Although I was unable to locate Dr. Elgamal's response, it appears that he requested additional information. Robert hastened to provide it with another fax on May 18:

"Dear Dr. Elgamal:

"On May 16 I faxed you copies of the reports of total bone scan and CT scan of abdomen and pelvis, both dated March 23, 1999. Herewith I am pleased to send you the previous year's reports on total body bone scan and CT scan of abdomen and pelvis as of September 2, 1998, to which reference was made in the March 23, 1999 reports. I am having a CBC study prepared by Omega Medical Labs and hope to send this to you next week.

Sincerely,
Robert Alexander"

On May 26, he sent the following letter to Earl Twiss, one of his colleagues in the Pennsylvania Prostate Cancer Coalition, to update him on his progress. It reflected some hopeful optimism.

"Dear Earl:

"Enclosed is a copy of the letter I received from Dr. Elgamal regarding their CaPVax Protocol # DC1-HRPC. There are two studies ongoing (as we speak) at UCLA and at MD Anderson. Another trial is to open up later this summer or early fall on the east coast, probably Washington DC area.

"The exciting part of this is what you'll read on page 29ff. It describes dendritic cells and the dramatic results from their vaccine thus far. Very interesting. I have sent him all the CT scans and a later CBC study with values closer to what he cites in his letter. I'm going to continue this dialogue with him.

"Incidentally, Dr. Sewell called me this morning to talk about my CT scan and the lymph node situation. He wants me to see Dr. Gordon about an angiogenesis therapy which he feels is quite exciting. He also said if I didn't qualify for that, he'd like to offer a bit of radiation to unclog the lymph system.

Most sincerely,
Robert"

However, it appears that the information he submitted did not qualify Robert for the trial. But with bulldog tenacity, he persisted with another fax on June 1:

"Dear Dr. Elgamal:

Re: CaP Vax Protocol # DC1-HRPC

"Thank you for your fax message of May 15 calling attention to the laboratory report from U.Va. of 02/19/00, which reflected low levels in RBC, Hemoglobin and Hematocrit profiles. At that time, I was just recovering from bronchitis. No doubt that may have had a definite effect on these values.

"Herewith is the latest CBC from Omega Laboratories, dated 05/22/00, which shows some improvement in RBC, Hemoglobin and Hematocrit values. Dr. Tierney has just prescribed some nutritional supplements for me which I feel will improve these values so as to meet your eligibility criteria.

"I am hopeful we can continue our dialogue and do look forward to hearing from you about the possibilities of my being included in a trial (or trials) of the protocol here on the East Coast or elsewhere.

With best regards,
Robert Alexander"

I had not received any e-mail correspondence from Robert since January, but I continued to call him every few weeks to see how he was doing. In one of our conversations he mentioned that lymphedema had slowed him down a bit, but he assured me that it was being addressed.

Then, after a five-month hiatus, I found myself on the short list of recipients of two forwarded e-mail messages from him, one on the Fourth of July and another on the 21st. His original compositions had ceased. These were the last e-mail messages I received from my friend.

On July 28, Robert underwent another round of CT and bone scans, under the advice of his primary physician, then met with him about a week later. The results were devastating. His cancer had metastasized to his thighs, his spine and his ribs. Fully aware of his condition, Robert declined to have any radiation treatments or chemotherapy. The formal written report of the tests was delivered a couple of days later. Gerda still has it, with a Post-It note affixed by Robert: "God is good…all the time!"

Robert's extended family on the East Coast had planned a birthday party for him in Lancaster on August 11. He and Gerda went through with it as planned. They were the only ones who knew the severity of his condition. But Gerda recalls someone noticing that Robert was missing the customary sparkle in his eyes.

Four days later, on August 15, he sent the following fax message to Dr. Myers:

> "Hello Dr. Myers!
>
> "Just a follow-up to our recent phone conversation regarding the dendritic cell trials at M.D. Anderson. I have nothing new to report about that. I was waiting to get my CBC report and latest PSA. My primary care physician sent me for a CT scan and a bone scan in late July.

"Included with this fax are those two reports as well as the lab report for PSA and CBC. These are all pretty much self-explanatory.

"Obviously these reports are somewhat distressing, yet I am not dispirited. I am taking 12 PC SPES capsules per day which dosage I began two weeks ago after talking with Harry Pinchot at PCRI. Previously I had been taking nine capsules.

"Where do I go from here? They didn't schedule me for an appointment on my last visit.

"Very best wishes.....and 'Keep Smilin'!'

Sincerely,
Robert"

Ten days later, on August 25, 2000, he sent a four-page fax to Dr. Elgamal, seeking to be considered for another upcoming clinical trial. The cover sheet gives clear evidence of his worsening condition:

"Dear Dr. Elgamal:

Re: CaP Vax Protocol # DC1-HRPC

"When we last communicated, you asked that I arrange for new CT and bone scans of the abdomen and pelvic areas. These were recently done and I am sending the reports with this letter. They suggest the cancer is giving my immune defenses quite a battle. I continue to be optimistic, banking on an increase in my PC SPES dosage to bring my PSA down from 40.6.

"I'm including an updated CBC as well. The Hemoglobin is still low at 11.7. Dr. Tierney has given me supplements which should improve that. The TB skin test was done last week and appears to be negative. However, Dr. Binder wants to have that done again next week.

"I am hopeful we can resume our dialogue and do look forward to hearing from you about the possibility of my being included in the trial of the protocol at M.D. Anderson.

With best regards,

Robert Alexander"

Chapter 15: Taps[18]

Day is done
Gone the sun
From the lakes
From the hills
From the sky.

All is well,
safely rest.
God is nigh.
Fading light
Dims the sight.

And a star
Gems the sky,
Gleaming bright
From afar,
Drawing nigh.

Falls the night.
Thanks and
praise,
For our days,
Neath the sun,

Neath the stars,
Neath the sky,
As we go,
This we know,
God is nigh

Robert's condition continued to deteriorate. In an effort to provide some relief from his increasing pain, Gerda convinced him that they should try another visit to a health spa. However, by this time it was nearly November, and she sought a warmer climate than Michigan. She located the Hippocrates Institute in West Palm Beach, Florida and made arrangements for an extended stay. Robert insisted on driving, but, after the first day, said simply, "I don't want to drive any more." So Gerda drove the rest of the way.

The Hippocrates staff was both caring and professional, and the Alexanders made fast friends with several other patients. But Robert's body was now rejecting the raw, healthy foods that had bolstered his immune system earlier. He could only be fed warm soups. He began to experience difficulty urinating and had to be taken to a hospital emergency room. This ended their stay, and Gerda and

Robert began the long drive back to Pennsylvania. It took three days.

On November 20, 2000, Robert sent the following message in a card to Inge, a patient he had met at Hippocrates:

> "Newville, PA
>
> "Dear Inge,
>
> "Gerda and I wanted to let you, Elizabeth and Jody[19] know that we made it back to Pennsylvania, thank heavens, with the help of friends like yourself. We can't thank the three of you enough for your kindness in provisioning us for the car trip north. We made overnight stops at Melbourne, Savannah, and Rocky Mount, NC. In 3 days we were back home, which was a good thing because the catheter needed some attention once we hit home base. The provisions you provided helped greatly in seeing us through.
>
> "It was so thoughtful of you folks to befriend us. We hope the remainder of your stay at Hippocrates Institute was as delightful as the first few weeks we were with you. We will always remember your kindnesses as well as the expressions of love shown us by Annamarie, Brian, as well as Olga, and Barbara[20] at the fitness center. Our whole experience at Hippocrates was enhanced by the wonderful people there.

"Needless to say, coming north we have run into 'ice box' weather. But we feel much the better for having been in Palm Beach. We got back in time to vote in our own home county on November 7, so we at least know what the voting tally is here.

"Thank you so much for being our friends on the road. We both hope the remainder of your stay was beneficial to your health.

"I can tell you that our stay there gave me a good boost. I feel much stronger now and we are most thankful to the Lord for His healing. I'll always remember the advice Brian and Annamarie gave us before we left. They emphasized that problems with our physical health are reversible; it just takes time and caring touch to repair what we ourselves may have done to our bodies.

"We're on the mend and hope you have similarly experienced a fresh infusion of strength and energy.

"As we're about to celebrate Thanksgiving, may we extend our love and best wishes to you and yours.

Much love, joy and peace,
Gerda and Robert"

Despite the upbeat tone of the last few paragraphs, Robert knew better. Several days later, he and Gerda went to see Dr. Binder. He looked at Robert and said, "You've put up a good fight. Now it's time for hospice." Robert accepted it. He stopped all medications except for painkillers and began receiving hospice care in his home.

After conducting a careful search during their early months in Newville, Robert and Gerda had become members of Falling Spring Presbyterian Church in Chambersburg, Pennsylvania. A primary attraction had been their choir. When the choir director, David Wenerd, invited him to join, Robert didn't hesitate. But now Gerda foresaw a problem, since Falling Springs was twenty-five miles from their home. The Alexanders had often attended services and Bible studies at the neighboring Big Spring Presbyterian Church in Newville. They knew and liked the pastor at Big Spring, Rev. Bill Beck. Gerda quietly approached him and asked whether there was any possibility of transferring their membership while Robert was still alive. Rev. Beck graciously accommodated her request.

In early December, during one of my periodic phone calls to inquire about Robert, Gerda shared the news that he had begun hospice care. The following week, Ray Goff and I drove up to Newville from Annapolis to visit our friend. It was December 18, the first day that Robert was unable to get out of bed. Gerda had cautioned that we would not be able to stay with him much more than hour, but he welcomed us warmly, and we had a rich time of sharing and prayer. As we were preparing to leave, Gerda grabbed both of my hands and, in her endearing German accent, said, "Erik, we have had thirty-one years together, and they've been GOOD!"

A few weeks later, Robert was transferred to a care facility on the grounds of Green Ridge Village, a short distance from their home. This didn't stop the flow of visits from people he'd touched and who cared for him. These included a local Amish couple, who drove up in their horse and buggy on a cold, rainy day in early January.

Scott Warrick remembers his final visit with Robert:

> "The most memorable and enduring recollection of Robert was the last time I saw him before he passed away. My wife Pam and I visited him in the hospice facility along with his wife Gerda, who had told us he was heavily sedated with morphine and might not be conscious to recognize us and speak with us. When [we] entered the room, that appeared to be evident. However, within moments, he opened his eyes and said, 'There are my friends Pam and Scott.' I went to his bedside, bent over for our customary embraces, after which he grasped my hand and closed his eyes, never relaxing his grip. Robert held my hand for the entire duration of our visit. It was his way of saying farewell to me. He passed away the next day. I shall always remember that final meeting!"

Jim Small came to visit Robert often. On his last visit, Robert struggled to speak: "We should ……, we should…." Jim looked at his friend and responded, "Robert, you can't ***do*** anything. Therefore there's nothing you should be ***doing***. Accept it. It's grace!"

Jim is of the opinion that Robert always believed that he would beat prostate cancer. And Jim is convinced that he did, though not in the way that Robert might have imagined!

On Tuesday, January 16, with his loving Gerda at his side, Robert quietly closed his eyes and went home to be with his Lord. As the tributes poured in, Gerda began to realize the incredible reach of their shared ministry.

On a beautiful and wintry Saturday morning, January 20, 2001, the ground covered by a fresh blanket of snow, a throng assembled inside The Big Spring Presbyterian Church in Newville, Pennsylvania for "A Service of Witness to the Resurrection for Robert H. Alexander." And what a witness it was! It included hymns and Scripture readings which he had chosen. Remembrances of Robert were shared by Mary Lanning, a close friend, as well as two of Robert's "soul brothers," Jim Williams and Jim Small. Clergy from both the Falling Spring and Big Spring churches participated, as did the choir and organist from Falling Spring. Their anthem was Robert's beloved "Sing Me to Heaven," by Daniel Gawthrop, which he had so often included on cards to other choir members. It had become part of his identity. Among the many cards which Gerda received after the service was this message from Mary Cole:

> "In choir this week, we talked about how much we would miss him. Sometimes when we sing, we can feel the Holy Spirit at work in us, lifting us beyond what we can do. 'Sing Me to Heaven' is such a piece. The harmonies are

very difficult, and we feel unsure of ourselves. Jan Crudden commented, 'How like Robert to choose an anthem where we would really need the presence of the Holy Spirit to sing it!' As we moved through that anthem, 'Sing me a love song, a requiem, sing me to heaven,' Robert was very near to us. We couldn't hold back the tears and could hardly see our music. We all know he is out of pain now, filled with joy in his heavenly home."

Mark Papera added this postscript:

"Mixed feelings....

"Praise God who made it possible for sinners to enter His Kingdom! Praise Jesus Christ who, through His death on the cross satisfied God the Father's wrath — His holy and just response to sin — and made our sins white as snow! Praise Jesus Christ who, through His Resurrection made that same resurrection possible for those who call Him Lord! Robert was one who called Jesus Lord and Savior, who knew Him deeply and lived out his remaining years in service to Him, in response to knowing His eternal love and forgiveness! Robert's strength came from Him! Robert now resides with Jesus!

"It will not be the same earth with Robert no longer a physical part of it. There will be an empty spot in my heart where once a dear friend filled. No longer will I be able to share our common love for Jesus with him, nor his with me. No longer will we lift each other up when the other was down, nor celebrate each other's 'ups'. Such deep pain must exist for Gerda, that none of us can possibly know, who loved and cared for Robert. Such pain and loss must exist for all those with prostate cancer he helped through his ministry.

"Lord God Almighty, I pray for your child Robert, who dwells with you eternally now…I pray for the strength to share that joy…I pray for the pain and sorrow I must feel, for a time, only to be overcome with your help…I pray for the support from the local community that Gerda needs, that other families need, that friends need…I pray for the people, like Robert,..[who] have entered my life, [who] have departed my life, [whom] I have yet to meet, who provide a glimpse of You by their lives lived…I pray for the power of the Gospel to cause me, and others I share it with, to come to a loving knowledge of You and Your saving grace…I pray all these things in Jesus name…Amen."

Epilogue: "Finishing Well"

"They will still bear fruit in old age. They will stay fresh and green." Psalm 92:14: (NIV)
"I have fought the good fight, I have finished the race, I have kept the faith." 2 Timothy 4:7 (NIV)

In their Winter 1996 issue, the editors of *Contact* magazine chose as their theme, "Finishing Well: How to Make a Lasting Impact with the Rest of Your Life." It featured vignettes of a number of older business men in various callings, ranging in age up to eighty-five. Though most were retired from their careers, each had continued to use his gifts and talents to reach out and minister to others.

Robert Alexander was sixty-eight years old when he was given his terminal diagnosis. Already retired from his career in the insurance industry, he could have pursued a number of avenues. He could have focused solely on his personal well-being, seeking the best available treatment and keeping himself as comfortable as possible. He could have pursued legal redress to enlarge his estate for his beloved Gerda. He could have withdrawn from contact with others. But he did not. Instead, he got on his knees and prayed. And he felt that his Lord's answer was to use his affliction in a positive way to reach out and minister to others with whom he could now identify personally. This attitude was reflected not only in his psalms of encouragement, but also in the addresses he so frequently gave to support and advocacy groups. There was no way that Robert would not finish well!

Notes

Chapter 1: ***"What an Opportunity to Witness!"***

1. Stephen Brown, speaking to a Christian Business Men's Committee couples conference, reported in *Contact*, Vol. 51, No. 1.

Chapter 2: ***"It's Robert!"***

2. Excerpts of letter, dated July 14, 1960, from E. Gillet Ketchum, Supervisor of Reeducation at Pennsylvania Hospital, to R.H. Alexander.
3. A test that measures the amount of prostate-specific antigen (PSA) in serum. PSA is a glycoprotein (a protein with a sugar attached) found in prostatic epithelial cells. It can be detected at a low level in the blood of all adult men. The PSA level is greatly increased in most men with prostatic cancer but can also be increased somewhat in other disorders of the prostate. Normal values depend on age. Older men may have slightly higher PSA measurements than younger men but this doesn't necessarily mean they have cancer. In most laboratories a value of less than 4 nanograms per milliliter (ng/ml) is normal.

Chapter 3: ***"Jesus I Love You" (Psalm 1)***

4. "Grace Alone," by Scott Wesley Brown and Jeff Nelson. © 1998 Maranatha! Music.

Chapter 4: ***"Teach Me About Thy Cross, Dear Lord" (Psalm 2)***

5. LHRH agonist: A compound that is similar to LHRH (luteinizing hormone-releasing hormone) in structure and is able to act like it. LHRH is a naturally occurring hormone that controls sex hormones in both men and women. Thus, an LHRH agonist serves in a manner similar to LHRH to control the same sex hormones.
6. A reference to *My Utmost for His Highest*, a devotional booklet with meditations from Oswald Chambers. As for many other

Christians, this had become a regular part of Robert's and my respective daily devotional times.

7. An abbreviated reference to Promise Keepers.
8. Chambers, op. cit.
9. Green Ridge Village, the community where Robert and Gerda Alexander resided.

Chapter 5: ***"At Autumn: A Prayer for Jim" (Psalm 3)***

10. Chambers, op. cit., p. 212 (July 30)
11. "Knowing You (All I Once Held Dear)," by Graham Kendrick © 1994

Chapter 6: ***"Sing Me to Heaven" (Psalm 4)***

12. "Sing Me to Heaven," by Daniel Gawthrop, © 1991 Dunstan House, Stafford, VA

Chapter 10: ***"Discouragement" (Psalm 8)***

13. Robert had already met Dr. Strum previously at a prostate cancer symposium in Michigan and had read his published work.
14. The formula called PC SPES is composed of eight herbal extracts of which seven are from China and one is from the United States. It is composed of five roots, mushroom spores, a flower, and the saw palmetto berry. According to anecdotal reports from survivors taking PC SPES, they have been able to reduce their PSA, prolong their lives, and improve its quality, after other procedures have failed. These experiences may indicate that PC SPES appears to be an option at any stage of prostate cancer where the survivor finds himself in Stages A, B, C or D. (Information taken from web site www.ustoo.com) Note: *spes* is the Latin word for hope.
15. The time a patient is likely to survive following a diagnosis of prostate cancer is related to the Gleason score, which ranges from 2 to 10. The lower the score, the better the patient is likely to do, though general principles do not always apply to individual patients. By combining the patient's Gleason score, PSA level and the clinical stage estimated by the physician, it is possible to estimate the likelihood that the patient has localized or locally advanced prostate cancer of different types.

Chapter 12: ***"My Faith in You" (Psalm 10)***

16. Chambers, op. cit. (By this time, Robert seems to have become quite intimate with this author!)

Chapter 14: ***"Barnabas"***

17. From *Dumb Things Smart Christians Believe* by Gary Kinnaman, (c) 1999. Used by permission of Vine Books, an imprint of Servant Publications, P.O. Box 8617, Ann Arbor, MI, 48107, 1-800-458-8505.

Chapter 15: ***Taps***

18. The bugle music played at the end of each day at every military installation throughout the world and at every military funeral is the haunting song, "Taps." It's the song that gives us that lump in our throats and usually creates tears in our eyes. Reportedly, its origin dates to 1862 during the Civil War, when Union Army Captain Robert Ellicombe was with his men near Harrison's Landing in Virginia. The Confederate Army was on the other side of the narrow strip of land. During the night, Captain Ellicombe heard the moans of a soldier who lay severely wounded on the field. Not knowing if it was a Union or Confederate soldier, Captain Ellicombe decided to risk his life and bring the stricken man back for medical attention. Crawling on his stomach through the gunfire, the Captain reached the stricken soldier and began pulling him toward his encampment. When the Captain finally reached his own lines, he discovered it was actually a Confederate soldier, but the soldier was dead. The Captain lit a lantern and suddenly caught his breath and went numb with shock. In the dim light, he saw the face of the soldier. It was his own son. The boy had been studying music in the South when the war broke out. Without telling his father, the boy enlisted in the Confederate Army. The following morning, heartbroken, the father asked permission of his superiors to give his son a full military burial despite his enemy status. His request was only partially granted. Captain Ellicombe had asked if he could have a group of Army band members play a funeral dirge for his son at the funeral. The request was turned down since the soldier was a Confederate. But, out of respect for the

father, they did say they could give him only one musician. The Captain chose a bugler. He asked the bugler to play a series of musical notes he had found on a piece of paper in the pocket of the dead youth's uniform. This wish was granted. The haunting melody we now know as "Taps," used at military funerals and at the end of each day on US military bases, was born.

19. Elizabeth and Jody were fellow patients at Hippocrates.
20. Annamarie and Brian were the directors of Hippocrates; Olga and Barbara were on the center's staff.

About the Author

Erik Pettersen, a business development consultant and former nuclear submarine officer, was a close friend of Robert Alexander during the last eight years of his life. He and his wife, Linda, live in Annapolis, Maryland. They have two grown children.

Printed in the United States
705100002B